CREATING YOUR
AWE-MAZING NEW LIFE

WHO AM I NOW?

AFTER RETIREMENT

NEW HOUSE
PUBLISHING COMPANY

FAWN GERMER

First published in the United States of America by Newhouse Books, a division of Newhouse Publishing Co., New York, NY.

Other titles by Fawn Germer:
Hard Won Wisdom, Perigee Books, 2001
Mustang Sallies, Perigee Books, 2004
Mermaid Mambo, Newhouse Books, 2007
The NEW Woman Rules, Network Books, 2007
Finding the UP in the Downturn, Newhouse Books, 2009
The Ah-Hah! Moment, Strauss Books, 2010
Pearls, Newhouse Books, 2012
Work-life Reset, Boulevard Books 2015
Coming Back!, St. Martin's Press, 2021
Here Comes the Sun, Boulevard Books 2024

Printed in the United States of America
Paperback ISBN 978-0-9838772-6-4

www.fawngermer.com
Speaking and coaching information: info@fawngermer.com

(727) 467-0202

DEDICATION

To all of my friends who are in this with me.
Damn, how did that time fly so fast? And how much fun
can we have while we still have a few minutes left?

CONTENTS

"Getting old is a fascinating thing.
The older you get, the older you want to get."

—Keith Richards

"We live in a youth-obsessed culture that is constantly trying
to tell us that if we are not young, and we're not glowing,
and we're not hot, that we don't matter. I refuse to let a
system or a culture or a distorted view of reality tell me
that I don't matter. I know that only by owning who and
what you are can you start to step into the fullness of life.
Every year should be teaching us all something valuable.
Whether you get the lesson is really up to you."

—Oprah Winfrey

"We don't stop playing because we grow old.
We grow old because we stop playing."

—George Bernard Shaw

INTRODUCTION:

Hey There...

"Welcome to the next chapter of your life—a chapter brimming with endless possibility, new adventures, and the freedom to explore all that you are and all that you can be . . ."

Blah, blah, blah, blah, blah . . .
What a crock.

Some people dive gracefully into retirement freedom. Others do big, painful belly flops. I started writing this book after watching a few of my friends sink into that big black hole and knowing how little it would take for them to get it right if they would make a few attitude adjustments.

They'd lost themselves. One day, they had respect, purpose, a paycheck, and a place to go. The next, they had a wide-open calendar, no income, and no title. They felt adrift as they tried to navigate the extremes of emotions including excitement, trepidation, relief, uncertainty, and fear.

This transition challenges everything: your self-esteem, relationships, finances, health, emotions, and security. But it can also lead you to explore the parts of yourself that were backburnered or ignored because you had so many other responsibilities and distractions.

For many of us, work has been more than our paycheck; it's been a central part of our identity. Our routines, social circles, and even our sense of who we are have revolved around our careers. Stepping out of the workforce can be very uncomfortable because the structure and schedules that once kept us moving have suddenly vanished. Yes, we are free, but liberation can be as daunting as it is exhilarating.

This book project has been a learning experience for me. I want to give a big shout-out to ChatGPT. I did most of the writing and personal inventories. ChatGPT helped with quizzes, lists, and some of the take-out sections. When I needed to come up with a hundred things to do when you can't leave the house, I asked AI. I had no idea what to suggest because I'm still living a life where I'm rarely home. But with a query on my computer, poof! Artificial intelligence immediately had the answers.

But, AI doesn't have all the answers, and neither do I. *You* do. That's the point of doing the work that is in this book. Dig deep. Figure out who you are at this point in life and what you really want. Don't be passive about retirement! Design one that uses every minute you've got to live with life.

You don't have to figure everything out the day you retire. Transition takes a minute. Retirement gives you a chance to learn new skills, travel, volunteer, spend more time with loved ones, rediscover passions you left behind, and focus on your well-being.

You can passively sit on the couch or make a choice to take charge and turn your life into a meaningful adventure. It's your choice, and this is your moment. You are in the third act of your life, so let's fill it with endless discovery. You won't be here forever. Your moment is right now.

CHAPTER 1:

Now What?

Here you are, waking up with a calendar that is wide open—for the rest of your life. How exciting! You earned this freedom after a lifetime of hard work. But wait. Work gave you a lot. Routine. Purpose. Income. Social interaction. Status. A sense of accomplishment and worth. Without that, who are you? This transition can be confusing, depressing, and intimidating if you don't steer your emotions and actions toward a positive, determined effort to make this the happiest, most hopeful moment possible.

A great retirement doesn't just happen. You have to decide how you are going to define yourself, and then design how you are going to live. If daily rounds of golf or pickleball will fill your soul, this will be easy. But for a lot of us, making retirement work means finding new ways to create a routine and find purpose, social interaction, and identity. That might seem like a very tall order, but it doesn't have to be.

Are you willing to push yourself, try new things, and open yourself to other ways to boost your self-esteem? You might find that studying a new language, teaching a young person how to read, stretching yourself by sculpting, or actually writing the book you've always wanted to write may be a great moment of fulfillment that is as rewarding as some of your greatest career achievements.

If you don't transition easily and naturally, start plotting it out. What will you do with your day Monday? Tuesday? And the rest of the week? It can seem like way too much time—but if you do this right, it will soon seem like it's not nearly enough for all the things you want to do. You have time to have fun! To do everything you always wished you could do—but couldn't.

Do not make the mistake of being slow to embrace this opportunity because, let's face it, you are getting older. You don't know whether you have 40 years in front of you—or four. There are going to be surprises, and some won't be good. Your health is a wildcard. So is money. Your friends, children, and grandchildren may or may not be as available and involved as you'd hoped. People you care about will start dying. This is not a question of the life you are going to create next year. It's a question of what you are going to do today and tomorrow.

Get out of bed, get off the couch, turn off the TV, and put your phone down. Time is running out.

Do something! Do something fun! And if you have time, do something constructive! Figure out something that will give you joy and something that will stimulate your brain. Think about how you are going to put yourself in a situation where you actively connect with other people. Once you decide what you love doing, you will be surprised how little time you actually have.

My dad was great at this. In his 80s, he still plotted out every day. He had a list of everything he was going to do, from visiting my mom in the nursing home (he actually went four times a day) to going to the YMCA to swim to going to the grocery store and then to the car wash. He had a list of people he wanted to call. He scheduled time to send emails or letters. And every day, he studied new drugs and drug interactions because he was a registered pharmacist until the day he died. Keeping up with the latest drugs and technology gave him purpose.

Dad would print out his daily list of things to do and put it in his shirt pocket so he always had a plan for what to do next. Because of my mom's Alzheimer's, he wouldn't leave town. He never felt right about doing fun things without her. That limited him, but he found a way to not let it limit his life.

That was a good lesson for me. We can waste so much time watching television or getting lost on the internet. But when we have a plan and places to go, we don't waste that time. We treasure it as a commodity for the activities that will keep us engaged in life, happy, learning, and fulfilled. Doing that takes effort, and it is a choice. Find some way to make every day meaningful. Do not slide into a rut of inactivity just because you don't know what to do. There are so many options.

CHAPTER 2:

A Quiz:
How's It Going So Far?

L et's start by taking stock of your life today. These questions cover various aspects of life that can be impacted by retirement, such as social connections, mental and physical health, financial security, and personal fulfillment.

1. How often do you feel fulfilled in your daily activities?
- Never
- Rarely
- Sometimes
- Often
- Always

2. Do you have a daily routine that you follow?

- No, I do not have a routine
- I have a routine but rarely follow it
- I follow my routine sometimes
- I usually follow my routine
- I strictly follow my routine

3. How often do you engage in hobbies or activities you enjoy?

- Never
- Rarely
- Sometimes
- Often
- Always

4. How connected do you feel with friends and family?

- Not at all connected
- Slightly connected
- Somewhat connected
- Very connected
- Extremely connected

5. How often do you participate in social activities?

- Never
- Rarely
- Sometimes
- Often
- Always

6. Do you feel financially secure in your retirement?

- Not at all
- Slightly
- Somewhat
- Very
- Completely

7. How often do you exercise or participate in physical activities?

- Never
- Rarely
- Sometimes
- Often
- Always

8. How do you rate your overall physical health?

- Very poor
- Poor
- Fair
- Good
- Excellent

9. How do you rate your overall mental health?

- Very poor
- Poor
- Fair
- Good
- Excellent

10. Do you feel a sense of purpose or meaning in your life?

- Not at all
- Slightly
- Somewhat
- Very
- Completely

11. How often do you feel lonely?

- Always
- Often
- Sometimes
- Rarely
- Never

12. Do you feel you have enough activities to keep you occupied?

- Not at all
- Slightly
- Somewhat
- Mostly
- Completely

13. How satisfied are you with your current living situation?

- Very dissatisfied
- Dissatisfied
- Neutral
- Satisfied
- Very satisfied

14. How often do you feel stressed or anxious?

- Always
- Often
- Sometimes
- Rarely
- Never

15. Do you feel you have a good balance between rest and activity?

- Not at all
- Slightly
- Somewhat
- Mostly
- Completely

16. How often do you try new things or learn new skills?

- Never
- Rarely
- Sometimes
- Often
- Always

17. Do you feel valued and appreciated by others?

- Not at all
- Slightly
- Somewhat
- Very
- Completely

18. How often do you volunteer or help others in your community?

- Never
- Rarely
- Sometimes
- Often
- Always

19. Do you have goals or plans for the future?

- Not at all
- Slightly
- Somewhat
- Very
- Completely

20. Overall, how satisfied are you with your retirement so far?

- Very dissatisfied
- Dissatisfied
- Neutral
- Satisfied
- Very satisfied

Scoring System

Each answer will be assigned a point value as follows:

Questions 1, 3, 5, 7, 11, 14, 16, 18:

- Never / Always: 1 point
- Rarely / Often: 2 points
- Sometimes: 3 points
- Often / Rarely: 4 points
- Always / Never: 5 points

Questions 2, 4, 6, 8, 9, 10, 12, 13, 15, 17, 19, 20:

- Not at all / Very dissatisfied: 1 point
- Slightly / Dissatisfied: 2 points
- Somewhat / Neutral: 3 points
- Very / Satisfied: 4 points
- Completely / Very satisfied: 5 points

Interpretation of Scores

Total Score: 20 - 40

- **Coping Poorly:** You may be struggling with the transition to retirement. Consider seeking support or making changes to improve your quality of life.

Total Score: 41 - 60

- **Coping Fairly:** You are managing the transition to some extent but may benefit from additional activities, social connections, or adjustments.

Total Score: 61 - 80

- **Coping Well:** You are adapting well to retirement, enjoying activities, maintaining connections, and feeling satisfied.

Total Score: 81 - 100

- **Coping Excellently:** You are thriving in retirement, feeling fulfilled, connected, and satisfied with your new lifestyle.

CHAPTER 3:

Life in Transition

Transition periods can feel incredibly uncomfortable and challenging. The uncertainty and disruption in your life now can lead to a lot of stress and anxiety. The routines and structures you once found comfort in got replaced by the unknown, and that can leave you feeling insecure and out of sorts.

One of the hardest parts about transitions is losing a sense of identity. Your career may have given you meaning, and your title may have given you respect from others. Now there is no job and no title. You might struggle with figuring out who you are without that professional role. The daily routine that used to give you purpose and a sense of achievement is suddenly gone, leaving a void.

Then there's the ambiguity. It's mentally exhausting to navigate new circumstances without a clear guide. The future feels uncertain, and that can be scary. You start doubting your ability to adapt, which only fuels your anxiety. The fear of the unknown and the possibility of "failing at retirement" can make the transition even more uncomfortable.

Social dynamics add another layer of discomfort. Changes in social circles can be daunting, and it can be tough finding and building new relationships. You might feel isolated and lonely not seeing or interacting with your colleagues every day. Finding new connections and a sense of community takes time, and during that period, the feeling of alienation can be overwhelming.

The physical and emotional stress that comes with transitions shouldn't be underestimated either. Adjusting to new routines, environments, or expectations is exhausting. The emotional toll of leaving behind what's familiar and comfortable can lead to grief and nostalgia, making the adjustment process even harder.

Transitions are a natural part of life and can bring growth and new opportunities, but they're undeniably tough. Acknowledging these feelings and seeking support can help make the journey a bit easier and pave the way for a smoother adjustment. Remember, it's okay to feel uncomfortable during these times—it's all part of the process.

"Don't try to be young. Just open your mind. Stay interested in stuff. There are so many things I won't live long enough to find out about, but I'm still curious about them. You know people who are already saying, 'I'm going to be 30— oh, what am I going to do?' Well, use that decade! Use them all!"
— Betty White

"My face carries all my memories. Why would I erase them?"
— Diane Von Furstenberg

"The longer I live, the more beautiful life becomes."
— Frank Lloyd Wright

"In retirement, the only identity you need to reclaim is the one you had before the world told you who you should be."
— Unknown

CHAPTER 4:

Soul Identity

You are not your job. You never were, but you spent so much time and energy on your career that it seemed all-important.

So if your identity was wrapped around what you did for a living, get ready for a great big gift from the universe. Your identity always was about what was going on inside of you, *who* you were as a human being, and *how* you interacted with your spirituality, nature, and other people.

Throughout this book, you'll be doing exercises that call on you to "go deep" and really explore who you are on a soul level. Don't rush through these questions. They are prompts. If you don't have enough space, keep writing elsewhere. This is like intensive psychotherapy that you can perform on yourself so you can discover and appreciate who you are as a human being. Do a few questions at a time, then come back to them.

Discovering Your Soul Identity, Part I

It's time to start going deep as you explore your soul identity. Self-exploration is a journey of growth, resilience, and self-compassion. Trust the process, and remember: every step forward is a step toward clarity, purpose, and a deeper connection with yourself.

1.   How do you feel about the aging process?

2.   How do you feel about yourself when you look in the mirror and see the older you?

3.   How did people treat you differently after 40? After 50? After 60? After retirement?

4.   How has that impacted your self-esteem?

5.   Has the way others have treated you affected your self-image?

6.   Do you feel a little pissed off?

7.   What are some examples of feeling "less than" because of your age?

8.   Do you feel like you are ignored or invisible? How does that feel?

9.   How have these changes made you feel about yourself?

10.   What stresses you these days?

11.   How have you learned to accept, cope, and adapt to changes relating to aging?

12.   How is your health? Have you had to deal with any health complications? How are you coping?

13.   By now, you've watched friends deal with their own health issues and even mortality. How has this affected you? What have you learned from them?

14.   Have you lived every day to the fullest? What could you have done to better embrace the possibility of every day, and what can and will you do to do a better job of that?

15. What are three of the happiest moments in your life? Describe them, how you felt at the time, and how you feel now looking back on them? How can you find opportunities to replicate that?

CHAPTER 6:

Using Affirmations as a Self-Help Intervention

If someone had told my younger self that I would wind up repeating positive affirmations regularly, much less teaching tens of thousands of people to do it, too, I would have told them they were out of their mind. In my first career, I was a professional cynic—an investigative reporter—and to me, affirmations sounded like a whole lot of garbage.

But they aren't.

Think of your brain working like a computer hard drive. It's programmed one way—in our brain's case, the programming occurs as we think the same thoughts over and over again. For those of us who say negative things about ourselves (everybody does), that programming can be pretty deeply ingrained. But here's the miracle in all of this: The brain's hard drive can be wiped clean and rewritten. If you repeat positive affirmations enough times, you will start to believe them—as long as your mind is receptive.

Many studies have proven this to be true. Let's say you tell yourself, "I am rapidly losing weight and looking thinner and thinner," and you repeat it over and over and over and over. Studies show that you will actually start to lose weight without consciously changing your eating behavior. The trick is repetition over time. When you stop repeating the positive affirmations, your old thoughts will creep back in because they've been there longer. All you have to do is continue repeating the positive affirmations.

But, as I mentioned, you have to be receptive to them. When my mother died, I wrote affirmations to help me quickly manage my grief and get on with my life. I learned then that there was no way to program my pain away. I had to go through it. My dad passed away two months after my mom, and so the only "affirmation" I could buy into was from that old song, *Feeling Stronger Every Day*. The line goes, "Knowing that you would have wanted it this way, I do believe I'm feeling stronger every day." It was so powerful because it was a simple affirmation that I repeated thousands of times. I *was* getting stronger every day. Who knew you could find a great affirmation in a song lyric?

Affirmations work in partnership with our subconscious mind. They help reframe negative thought patterns. By consciously focusing on positive statements, we move our attention away from self-doubt or limiting beliefs and hone in on other thoughts that affirm our strength and potential.

The magic is in the repetition. I tell people to say every affirmation 25 to 50 times a day for two weeks, then ten times a day for two weeks, and after that, as needed. Affirmations can absolutely boost our resilience and self-confidence. This can be really helpful during challenging times or when facing health issues. I have used affirmations to deal with breakups, weight challenges, family drama, and professional challenges like deadlines and concentration. Heck, I once used them (successfully) to get me to stop speeding.

We will use them here in this program because they can be some of the most impactful tools in your arsenal.

Affirmations for Your New Life as a Retiree

- I embrace this new chapter of my life.
- My heart is filled with excitement and positivity.
- I easily adapt to change and find joy in each day.
- I am open to new things.
- I earned and deserve this time to relax, rejuvenate, and enjoy life.
- I am creating a meaningful and fulfilling life.
- I focus on living in the present moment, and I am hopeful about the future.
- I am open to new passions, hobbies, and talents that bring me happiness.
- I am grateful for the financial security and freedom that retirement provides.
- I focus on solutions and positive outcomes, knowing worry serves no purpose.

CHAPTER 7:

Step One:
Get Outa the House

All you need to do to shake things up is leave the house. But for a lot of people, that simple yet powerful action is one scary step. It's easy to get comfortable with what is familiar, but the longer you settle into that space, the deeper your rut becomes.

Are you open to the world around you? This is not just about going somewhere; it's about embracing the idea that life outside is rich with possibility. Whether it's a walk in the park, a coffee with a friend, or a visit to a museum, each time you push beyond your boundaries, you have the chance to connect with others, be active, and discover something new. The fresh air, the change of scenery, and the simple act of being among people can be incredibly invigorating.

Imagine starting your day with a walk through a local garden or along a scenic trail. The beauty of nature, the chirping of birds, and the rustle of leaves underfoot can refresh your mind and spirit. Or consider joining a community group, attending a class, or taking up a new hobby. Meeting new people who share your interests can spark joy, creativity, and a renewed sense of purpose. These connections can lead to lasting friendships and provide the kind of social interaction that is vital for emotional well-being.

But those opportunities are not going to come to you. You have to leave the house. Whether you're traveling to new places, volunteering for causes close to your heart, or simply exploring your area, every outing adds to the richness of your post-work life. The more you do it, the more confident you become.

Step out into the world with curiosity and enthusiasm, and you'll find that life outside is not just waiting for you—it's welcoming you with open arms.

CHAPTER 8:

Let's Get Moving!

It's time to get outa your head *and* outa the house. We'll continue your deep dive into your soul identity, but it's time for you to have a little fun RIGHT NOW.

Here's a list of 100 things you can do *this week* to get you busy and make you happier *right now:*

- Plan or take a trip
- Join the YMCA
- Take up gardening
- Learn a new language
- Volunteer at a local charity
- Take a cooking class
- Join a gym
- Attend local events
- Join a book club
- Learn photography

- Take up knitting, quilting, sewing, or crocheting
- Visit museums and volunteer for them
- Take a spontaneous road trip
- Go hiking
- Join a walking group
- Start a journal
- Learn to play an instrument
- Take online courses
- Attend workshops or seminars
- Go fishing
- Try bird-watching
- Start a small business
- Visit family and friends
- Take up yoga
- Join a meditation group
- Attend community meetings or your city council
- Volunteer at a school
- Take a cruise
- Join a choir
- Get involved with community theater
- Explore local parks
- Take up cycling, skiing, or another sport
- Visit historical sites
- Take up pottery, painting, or sculpting
- Go camping
- Start a DIY project
- Visit farmers' markets
- Play golf
- Attend fitness classes

- Try new recipes
- Visit new restaurants
- Go to movies
- Take up scrapbooking
- Join a card, chess, or board game club
- Volunteer at an animal shelter
- Start a podcast
- Attend local festivals
- Join a travel club
- Study genealogy
- Take dance lessons
- Volunteer at a hospital or nursing home
- Join a wine-tasting club
- Visit botanical gardens
- Take up martial arts
- Attend local lectures
- Visit zoos and aquariums
- Take up sailing
- Volunteer at a food bank
- Start a YouTube channel
- Attend local sports events
- Take up beekeeping
- Visit amusement parks
- Create a fitness routine
- Visit your library and volunteer there
- Join a cultural club
- Visit local landmarks
- Volunteer for a mentoring program
- Attend local art shows

- Take up scuba diving or snorkeling
- Volunteer at a community center
- Visit local breweries
- Take up glassblowing
- Volunteer at a soup kitchen
- Attend local workshops
- Attend local music festivals
- Join a running group
- Learn skiing, diving, kayaking, or paddleboarding
- Volunteer at a children's center
- Volunteer at a community garden
- Go to comedy shows
- Pick up an instrument and join a community orchestra
- Attend local poetry readings
- Volunteer at a crisis center
- Do things you haven't tried—an obstacle course, hot air ballooning, white-water rafting, archery, zip-lining, bungee jumping, skydiving, etc.
- Volunteer at a senior center
- Join a writing group
- Join a local improv group
- Volunteer at an environmental organization
- Attend local film festivals
- Go to the planetarium
- Volunteer at a veterans' organization

If you can't find something to do after looking at that list, you've got to admit that you are not trying. The issue is simple: Do you want an exciting, challenging, stimulating, and fulfilling retirement, or don't you? You have to make that choice. You decide whether you will redefine yourself by default or design. If you do it by default, you can bet you will doom yourself to a boring, pointless existence. You can try that, I guess, but remember: You are running out of time. Why *not* find a vibrant life instead of waiting for it to find you?

CHAPTER 9:

Getting Your Mojo Back

A study from the AARP found that, while most retirees planned for financial facets of retirement, nearly 60 percent put no effort into preparing for their emotional needs in retirement. That same study said almost half never pondered what they would need to do to continue to feel fulfilled.

Their most common complaints were boredom, isolation, loneliness, and/or a lack of purpose. They struggle with a feeling that they are no longer needed. Work is such a primary source of identity.

Even for those who didn't like their jobs, work gave them a reason to get up every morning. But, over time, you can find your tribes that will give you new reasons to get up. You can have a "tribe" for any of your interests. I've got my "Swim Tribe" at the Y, my "Kayaking Tribe," my "Camping Tribe," and my "Hanging Around Town Tribe." It took time and effort to build those tribes, and it is made easier by having a phone or text list for each group so I can set up get-togethers.

It's important not to wait to get invited to things because people are always waiting for someone to take the lead to bring them together. I am generally that person, and that does not bother me in the slightest. I know some people are insulted when they don't get reciprocal invitations from others, but it is just reality. People suck at inviting and reciprocating. So take the lead.

After the initial years of adjustment, the AARP found that most retirees (72 percent) feel relaxed, 64 percent say they are happy, and 59 percent say they love their freedom. It is interesting that one in six are still working in some capacity, whether part-time or full-time, and nearly one in four do regular volunteer work.

Some people glide easily into retirement, quickly embracing their new freedom and identity. But a lot of people struggle with it. Take a long, deep breath and remind yourself that retirement is a new chapter, not the end of the book. You've got plenty of pages left to write. You have so much to explore.

For example, my friend Patty Ivey decided to learn to play the bass guitar with YouTube videos as her guide, and guess what? She's *great* at it. She and her drummer husband are always playing gigs around the area.

If you dive into your freedom—really dive into it—you'll get to the point where you wonder how you ever had time to go to work.

Embrace spontaneity! Say "yes" to new experiences and opportunities that come your way. Shake things up a little every day. Try things you've never tried or secretly wished you could. Volunteer for a cause that sparks your passion. Giving back not only helps others, but it also reminds you of the value you bring to the table. Plan a getaway. Travel! Whether it's a weekend road trip or an exotic vacation, exploring new places can open your mind and refresh your spirit. Dive into the world of books. Whether it's fiction, nonfiction, or self-help, losing yourself in a good read can provide inspiration and fresh perspectives.

Get moving! Exercise, dance, or take a walk out in nature. Your body and mind will thank you. Connect with old friends and make new ones. Laughter and shared memories are the best medicine for an identity crisis.

Some things can be done on your own. Embrace your inner artist. Pick up a pen and start journaling. Reflecting on your thoughts and experiences can bring clarity and self-discovery. Embrace your inner artist. Paint, sculpt, write poetry, or express yourself in any creative way that feels right to you. Challenge yourself intellectually. Take up a new course or engage in thought-provoking discussions with friends. Keep those mental gears turning! Take care of yourself. Prioritize self-care activities like bubble baths, meditation, or indulging in your favorite guilty pleasure. Spruce up your surroundings. Rearrange the furniture, redecorate a room, or create a cozy nook where you can unwind and be yourself.

You've done amazing things, and those achievements are still a part of you. Share your wisdom. Become a mentor or coach to someone younger or less experienced. Your guidance and expertise can make a meaningful impact.

Explore entrepreneurship. Got a business idea or a skill you can monetize? Start your own venture and let your entrepreneurial spirit soar. Embrace technology. Connect with loved ones through video calls, explore online communities, or learn how to use that gadget you've been eyeing. Pursue lifelong learning. Expand your knowledge by taking online courses or attending workshops on subjects that intrigue you. Learning is a lifelong adventure!

Finally, remember to be kind to yourself. Embracing change takes time, so be patient, celebrate small victories, and enjoy the journey.

CHAPTER 10:

Discovering Your Soul Identity, Part II

It's time to keep going deep into your soul identity. You are uncovering truths that matter. Each reflection brings you closer to understanding yourself and embracing the changes life brings.

1. Describe a typical day in your life now, what you like about it, and what you don't.

2. What would you like your typical day to be? What can you do to manifest that?

3. Who are your closest friends? How have they helped you as you face this next phase in your life? What role do they play, and how would you like to involve them?

4. Design a "cabinet" of friends, colleagues, mentors, and people you respect who can help you design this next phase of your life. What are their strengths, and how can those strengths be used to help you? What could they do for you if you were to ask for any and all favors?

5. It's okay to feel lost. Feel it. Unless you feel it, you can't move to the next step. Do you feel adrift? Misplaced? At sea? Give voice and validation to your feelings. You are allowed to feel anything that you feel. Hiding from your feelings does not make those feelings go away. So feel them. Write them down. Acknowledge them. Doing that is the first step toward discovering your soul's truth.

6. How has a need for control affected your life? Do you ever feel in control? How do you feel now? How do you make peace with situations that are out of your control? Are you at a point in life where you want to or can let go of some of that need for control? Write about the good and bad influence of control in your life.

7. Take a moment to review the times in life when you had to face significant change. How did you adapt? What did you learn? How would you coach someone to accept change? Can you use those skills now?

8. Write down three thoughts you have never shared with anyone.

9. Write about your worries. What worries you about today, next year, and the next five years? What worries you about the rest of your life?

10. Ponder the Dalai Lama's quote on worry. "If you can do something about a situation, why worry? And if you can't do something about a situation, why worry?" Worry is of no use.

11. Who are you without your career identity?

12. A healthy body is a perfect body. Over the years, has your weight or body image affected your self-esteem or limited you from doing things you might have enjoyed? How did any negative energy concerning your weight affect you, and how can you keep it from doing that in your future?

13. Write your obituary.

14. Now write your obituary with no reference whatsoever to your career.

15. Are you taking care of your body? Most of us have to work to earn a pleasant aging process, so are you doing your part? What are you doing right? Wrong? What could you do better? What kind of commitment are you willing to make to take care of yourself? What is your action plan?

16. What has inspired you about the others you have watched age? Who are your aging heroes? What did you learn from them? How are you using that in learning to grow?

17. How do you feel about your changing looks? What do you see when you

look in the mirror? What do you say to yourself when you see signs of aging? Are you loving yourself as you do this?

18. By now, you have watched people you care about face illness and die. What have you learned from watching them? How did it impact you? How did you recover? How has the experience impacted your perspective and the way you live?

19. What do you fear about getting older? Why do you have these fears? How likely are they to manifest?

20. How did you treat older people when you were in your 20s, 30s, and 40s? Is payback a bitch?

CHAPTER 11:

The Self-Esteem Gut Punch

Your self-esteem can take a huge hit in the days following your last day of work. Our adult lives have been structured around work, and so many of us take pride in what we do and who we do it for.

"What do you do?" is the most common and reliable icebreaker when meeting new people. It's also a bit unfair because it helps us to tag and judge people. We decide a lot by how they answer that question, and now, your answer to that question is a shrug. What *do* you do? They aren't asking what you did. You aren't far from the point where most people do not care one bit about what you took so much pride in for your entire life.

My friend, George, explained this to me. There comes a point when you realize that you have been tossed into the pile of used and unneeded people. I'd say that is unnecessarily negative, but having spent most of my life in Florida where we have so many retirees, I have watched it happen over and over. People who were accomplished, respected, and even revered are reduced to the title of "old person," or "older people" as they now say to be politically correct.

I've seen it happen to surgeons and government leaders, famous entertainers, CEOs, accomplished business owners, teachers, nurses, professors, scientists, engineers, social workers, journalists, researchers, military leaders, and every kind of professional who delivered—really delivered—every day of their lives. The point comes when nobody asks or wants to hear about their careers. There is a solution, and we'll get to that in a minute.

Complicating this is that many people end up having to retire when they don't want to. They may be laid off, eased out, or outright pushed out because of the economy, a merger, forced retirement age, leadership change, or that old "We're going in a new direction" line. These people may feel they still have so much more to give, but nobody seems to want it. After a full career of success and recognition, they get screwed.

If you are an "older person" and your career ended abruptly or before you were ready, it's really hard to accept because there's probably not going to be a big comeback performance of the same significance. You probably are aging out. While some enlightened companies *want* older professionals, a lot aren't so open and appreciative.

You can let this make you bitter, or you can do the healthiest thing, which is to find a way to accept it. Decide for yourself that you will embrace the best parts of your soul self that you never really explored or honored when you were so busy defining yourself by your work.

You can prop yourself up by knowing you are not alone. Transamerica just reported that 56 percent of all retirees said they retired sooner than they'd planned. Almost half of them said they were forced or eased out. So the insult of your abrupt career end was likely not about you or your performance, even if your employer framed it that way. It's what happens to too many people at this point in life. The sad reality of our society is that it treats older people pretty damn crappy. It is infuriating, but we do not have time to waste being miserable about it.

I met a miserable man at a party a few weeks ago. He'd been pushed out of his job at a multinational financial services company 12 years ago. He was desperate to tell his story to someone who hadn't heard it, and it took way too long for him to tell me the details. Listening to him recite the story and revisit his anger took at least 20 minutes. He was stuck in his resentment. He wanted that company to apologize to him, to miss him and his substantial talents, and to see (and regret) the terrible mistake it had made by casting him out. His wife was embarrassed by what he was doing and tried to pull him away, but he did not want to stop. For years, he has groused about the horrible thing that happened to him. "Dude," I finally said, "they stopped thinking about you the day you left. The people who did it probably don't even work there anymore." He admitted he knew that was true. "So," I asked, "who are you punishing by thinking about it every day, 12 years later? They don't even remember you were there. What is this doing for you?" "Nothing," he said. "But I had the best performance record for . . ." and he launched into another speech about why the company had done him wrong.

Don't be that guy. It is so hard to swallow injustice, but we are at an age where we have to spend our time in joy, not anger. It's especially hard to do that when what happened impacts your financial future. None of us knows how long we will get to enjoy our health and freedom. But we are always one day closer to the day when someone tells us to hand over our keys because we can no longer drive. We don't have time to waste being miserable.

It's a hard reality, but when we leave a job, life goes on without us. You're lucky if they remember that you were once there, but at some point, they won't.

I left a job after eight years as a reporter for a newspaper in Colorado. I gave so much of myself to that place. But the day after I left, guess what? The newspaper still came out. It came out the next day, too, and then the day after that. It came out for years until the place went out of business like so many newspapers. But it was clear, as much as I gave to that newspaper, it didn't need me to continue on. Generations before I ever worked there, there were a number of men who devoted themselves to that newspaper who revered it so much that they actually had their ashes encased in the lobby of the building! The sad part of the story is, nobody cared. The ashes were joked about. Then the paper relocated, and I think the company at least had the ashes put in the ground somewhere. But that pretty much says it all. You can give and give and give and give, but when you are gone, the company moves on without you. Like the saying goes, "The business won't love you back."

Whether you left under great terms or bad terms, that part of your life is over, and the faster you accept it, the faster you can create a magnificent new life. If your exit from the workplace still doesn't sit right with you, you can choose to stay stuck like the guy at the cocktail party or forgive whatever you may think is unforgivable just so that you can move on, love yourself, and love this moment.

There is a very important quote that is misattributed so much, I don't know who said it, but it wasn't me. "Forgiveness is a gift that you give to yourself."

We have to forge ahead with the strongest self-esteem we can muster. We can't do that if we are held back by anger, resentment, or regret. You are going to live a spectacular life—no matter what. As some would say, F* 'em. If you are healthy, you have so much to be grateful for. Don't waste these good, healthy days with bitterness, resentment, and self-loathing. These are the good days! Live them.

Work fills our time with challenge, reward, intrigue, and even a little drama. While we are in that world, it feels so important and all-consuming—even when we have other things we value more. You may have had a job, but also a family, a relationship with God, your own interests, fitness, and volunteer efforts that may have been important to you, but work always took the most time, It had to seem "bigger" in some ways. With that gone, who are you? Who are you going to be without that title?

Are you any less of a smart contributor to society? Are you any less valuable because you don't have that job? No! God/the universe never cared what you did for a living. God/the universe cared what you did for the world. Lucky you, you have plenty of time now to focus on what you can do to help others and do more to make the world better.

I've interviewed many accomplished and famous people and leaders who admitted their self-esteem struggles. Hearing them share insecurities about their looks, weight, or even competence was shocking. I thought they had it all together. I assumed that the reward for huge success was boundless self-esteem. But it wasn't.

How could the people we revere put themselves down like we do? It made me realize that most of the negativity we feed ourselves is a bunch of garbage. It's not true. If I hear that going on in my head, I tell myself, "That is not true."

Regardless of what you did or how people treated you, and regardless of what you're doing now and how you think people are seeing or treating you, you are a whole, deserving, and valuable person. You are just as good as anybody else. There will be times when you don't get the respect you think you deserve. Shrug it off. If younger people are dismissive, just feel sorry for them. They will get their turn as well if they are lucky to live as long as you.

You can make a case that society does not treat older people well. But we have the power to treat ourselves well. We can wake up every day and see ourselves as whole, interesting, and vibrant contributors to society. So what if you don't have the job title you used to have? The best title you can ever attain on this earth is "good person." Focus on that. Celebrate that. If you fill your days with goodness, you are a vital member of society. Remind yourself that matters and you matter.

I don't need other people to validate that I'm a good person. I know that on the inside. I work on it every day. That's what makes me valuable and gives me purpose. That's what will matter most when I leave this earth. It is more important that I was good on the inside—that I was there for other people and grew even better over time. That is so much more important than my career as an author, speaker, and journalist. I get to work on what really matters in life—no matter how old I am.

You don't get a do-over on this day or any day, so you might as well live it large and love yourself every minute. You are valuable to the fabric of a society that is, let's face it, kind of coming unglued. So be a contributor with goodness. Fight hate. Spread love. That's the most important job you've got and the most important job you have ever had.

Another thing is that, at this point in life, none of us looks as good as we once did. When you look in the mirror and see yourself getting older, it can be a little rough to handle. It sure is for me, because as an outdoorswoman, I spent every day in the sun and have the wrinkles to show for it. I wonder what I'm going to look like years from now. But I can't do anything about it. This is what I look like, it is my privilege to have lived such a spectacular, fun life in the sun, and I'm just going to have to accept it. I can make peace with it, get a bunch of fillers and a facelift (which I really don't want to do), or make myself miserable about it. That misery will only escalate because this face is only going to look older. I hold my head high and love myself today, no matter what.

I am a beautiful person living a beautiful life. And that, my friend, is a sign of good self-esteem.

Affirmations to Say Every Morning

- This is going to be a GREAT day!
- I am grateful for my health, my home, and all of the wonderful people in my life.
- I am proud of all I have accomplished and realize my greatest accomplishment will be growing into an even greater human being.
- I am excited to explore new passions and interests because I embrace this new chapter with an open heart and mind.
- I deserve to relax and enjoy this time in my life.
- I find joy and purpose in every single day.

- I make a positive difference.
- I am surrounded by love and support.
- My life is filled with positivity and good energy.

CHAPTER 12:

Discovering Your Soul Identity, Part III

You're doing important work by continuing this moment of self-discovery. Stay curious and open, knowing that every insight strengthens your understanding and empowers you to approach life's next chapter with confidence, purpose, and renewed energy.

1. When did you realize you were on the other side of middle age? Was it a rude awakening or were you just excited to get into retirement?

2. What are you afraid to tell others about your life and/or feelings? What does that say about how deep your feelings are? You don't have to tell the world what's going on inside of you, but write it down here for yourself.

3. Do you take it personally when you feel ignored or encounter discrimination or rejection because of your age? How does it feel? Do you see the same thing happening to others? Are you shouldering too much of the insult?

4. Tell the truth about your relationship. Are you happy? Are you settling? Are you with your soulmate? Spend some time looking at the relationship you are in, why you are in it, and if it is right for you.

5. What has been your life's defining moment? How did it shape and grow you?

6. What was the best advice you ever got and how did it impact your life? How does it impact you now?

7. What advice have you given others that you wish you could follow for your-self?

8. What is your spiritual connection, if any? How has it changed since your childhood? What phases have you gone through? What role does it play in your life now? How do you want to explore or grow a spiritual connection, if you have one, in the future?

9. What do you think happens at the end of the end? Is there life after death or nothing at all? How do you see that part of your future? How do you feel about it? Does that make it easier to face what stands between you now and crossing to the "other side?"

10. Do you have a mind that is mostly open or closed to new, perhaps strange ideas or concepts? Are you ready to really dive into new things that may have seemed "way out there"?

11. Write down 15 activities you really enjoy, whether they involve athletics, writing, traveling, exploring, gardening, cooking, etc. How often do you do these things? When was the last time you enjoyed them? Make a plan (with a timeline) for refocusing some of your time on doing activities that you love.

12. Do you feel safe? When do you feel most safe and when do you feel fear or vulnerability? What gives you those feelings? What can you do to create more security in your life? Explore the times in your life when you felt safe. What gave you that feeling?

13. Write down 50 things for which you are grateful.

14. Who are the negative influences in your life? How do they impact your life and your attitude? How can you tone down or tune out their negativity? Would you be happier eliminating these people from your life?

15. Do you have to overthink everything? Which of your challenges could you just abandon, leaving it to the universe to handle?

16. What were your best and worst decisions in relationships? Do you have many regrets in this area? What have you learned?

17. Have you had enough fun in your life? Could you have more? Any regrets?

18. What were your biggest time wasters in life? What are your biggest time wasters now? How could you better use that time? Can you consciously decide not to continue wasting this time?

19. If you were going to write a book, what would it be about? Why would you write that book? Write the first four paragraphs.

20. Do feel like you have to work, if not for the money, but for the soul? Talk about what work has meant and means now to you.

CHAPTER 13:

When Family Doesn't Fill the Void

Strong family bonds can make this chapter of life easier, but not everybody has them. I have one friend who retired after a visible, important career as a public official. He bought a huge mountain home and looked forward to regularly hosting his children and grandchildren. What he didn't expect was for the kids and grandkids to be busy. They rarely drove up there. They weren't mad at him, but they were just tied up with their own lives. He was crestfallen and felt disappointed and sad for years.

We can't control other people. We can't make them show up because we want them to show up. We can hope with all of our hearts that they do, but if they don't, we can either cry about it or go on living. It's a sad reality of life that people you have shown up for don't always show up for you. Good friends can really disappoint us, too. It is crushing, but I've always noticed that when someone doesn't show up, someone else—someone who I never expected—shows up instead. I always get what I need, but not always from the people I expected to get it from. So if your family lets you down, expand your circle.

In one especially low moment—my mom and dad had both just died and a long relationship had ended—one of my best friends ghosted me. Another friend didn't show up at all. I was devastated. But I met a woman who said, "Those people needed to get out of your life in order to make room for new, better people." Two years passed, and then I reflected on all of the people who had come into my life during that time without my old bestie. That woman had been right. New, *better* friends showed up in my life.

CHAPTER 14:

Growing Your Circle

One of the easiest ways to make new friends is to join Meetup.com and fill your calendar with group activities that you will love. Hopefully, you've heard about Meetup. If you haven't, it's not a dating site. Meetup is an online platform for groups to post groups and activities and find people with shared interests. It's a great place to network and make friends. There are more than 50 million members of Meetup.com, and I am one of them.

During the next four days, people in my area can go to meetups to eat tacos, do yoga, connect with other singles, go to a baseball game, discuss philosophy, go with people to Walt Disney World, go bowling, take a hike, enjoy happy hour, hang with a travel group, go for a bike ride, play pickleball, explore divorce recovery (or alcohol recovery for that matter), eat sushi, or go kayaking.

I joined a Meetup group more than a decade ago. It is The SLACKERS (Simply Laidback Adventurers, Campers, and Kayakers). We've gone on trips all over the world, and I've made lifelong friends in that group. It doesn't matter that many of us have been going to that club for years. The first thing we say when we see someone we don't know is, "Hi. My name is . . ." That is what Meetup is about.

Examples of Meetup Groups

- ·Book Clubs
- ·Hiking Groups
- Tech Meetups
- Language Exchange
- Wine Tasting Groups
- Yoga Classes
- Running Clubs
- Photography Clubs
- Board Game Nights
- Coding Bootcamps
- Fitness Bootcamps
- Singles Meetups
- Meditation Groups
- Cooking Classes
- Art Workshops
- Startup Incubators
- Travel Enthusiasts
- Writers Workshops
- Movie Buffs
- Dog Walking Groups
- Parenting Groups
- Investment Clubs
- Car Enthusiasts
- Dance Classes
- Volunteer Groups
- Music Jams
- Gardeners' Circles

- Amateur Astronomy
- Networking Events
- Sci-Fi Fans
- Historical Societies
- Homebrewing
- Environmental Activists
- Public Speaking Clubs
- Quilting Bees
- Theater Groups
- Mindfulness Meditation
- Motorcycle Clubs
- Spirituality Meetups
- Science Discussion Groups
- Comic Book Fans
- Photography Walks
- Bird-Watching
- Chess Clubs
- Knitting Circles
- Tennis Groups
- Martial Arts Classes
- Social Dancing
- Public Art Projects
- Genealogy Clubs
- Skiing and Snowboarding
- Potluck Dinners
- Language Learning
- Urban Exploration
- Carpool Groups
- Vegan Meetups

- Beer Tasting
- Beach Volleyball
- Sewing Circles
- DIY Projects
- Aquarium Enthusiasts
- Social Media Influencers
- Fishing Clubs
- Magic Groups
- Cybersecurity
- Spiritual Book Study
- Radio Control Aircraft
- Scrapbooking
- Fantasy Sports
- Survivalist Groups
- Concert Goers
- Fitness Challenges
- Weightlifting Groups
- Community Theater
- Film Production
- Puppet Making
- CrossFit Classes
- Fire Spinning
- Tiny House Enthusiasts
- Book Writing
- Wildlife Photography
- Roller Skating
- Trail Running
- Triathlon Training
- Historical Reenactment

- Card Games
- Cultural Festivals
- Mushroom Foraging
- Anime and Manga Fans
- Indie Film Clubs
- Tarot Reading
- Paragliding
- Astronomy Night
- Community Gardening
- Origami
- Urban Sketching
- Sailing Clubs
- Puzzle Solvers

CHAPTER 15:

Making Friends at Meetups

Now, if you are a bit of an introvert (like me), that first conversation can be a bit of a bear. So here is what I suggest you do to get things moving.

Introducing yourself is easy . . .
- "Hi, I'm [Your Name]. Nice to meet you."
- "Hello! How are you today?"

Breaking the ice . . .
- "How did you hear about this group?"
- "Have you been to this meetup/group/event before?"
- "What made you decide to come to this?"
- "What do you think of this setting/venue?"
- "Where are you from originally?"
- "Are you into any sports or fitness activities?"
- "What do/did you do for work?"
- "Do you have any exciting plans for the weekend?"

- "Got any big travel plans coming up?"
- "I really like your [item of clothing/accessory]. Where did you get it?"
- "You're really good at that [whatever it is they're doing]."
- "You have a great energy. It's been nice talking to you."
- "Your [work/idea] sounds really interesting."

Listening and Responding
- "That sounds fascinating. Tell me more about it."
- "Wow, that's impressive! How did you get started with that?"
- "I can relate to that. I've had a similar experience."
- "I see what you mean."
- "That sounds interesting."
- "Really? Tell me more about that."
- "I understand."
- "That must have been challenging/exciting/interesting."
- "Can you elaborate on that?"
- "What happened next?"
- "How did that make you feel?"
- "That reminds me of something similar I experienced."
- "That's a good point."
- "I hadn't thought of it that way."
- "Why do you think that happened?"
- "Thanks for sharing that with me."

Asking for Recommendations
- "Do you have any favorite restaurants or cafés around here?"
- "Can you recommend any good places to visit around here?"
- "What's your favorite local spot for [activity, food, etc.]?"

Wrapping Up

- "How'd you enjoy it?"
- "It was great meeting you. I hope we can chat again soon."
- "Thanks for the conversation. Enjoy the rest of your day/evening!"
- "I'm glad we met. Let's keep in touch."
- "Are you on Facebook/Instagram? It would be great to stay in touch."

Affirmations As You Make New Friendships

- I am open to new people and friendships.
- I radiate warmth and friendliness. People want to be around me.
- I am great at initiating conversations and finding common ground with strangers.
- I release fear and hesitation when I approach new social situations.
- People are attracted to my confidence and positive energy.
- I am curious about others and eager to learn from them.
- I listen much more than I talk.
- I attract like-minded people who appreciate my authenticity and kindness.

"When it comes to aging, we're held to a different standard than men. Some guy said to me: 'Don't you think you're too old to sing rock n' roll?' I said: 'You'd better check with Mick Jagger.'"
—*Cher*

"There are six myths about old age: 1. That it's a disease, a disaster. 2. That we are mindless. 3. That we are sexless. 4. That we are useless. 5. That we are powerless. 6. That we are all alike."
—*Maggie Kuhn, founder of the Gray Panthers movement*

"How old would you be if you didn't know how old you were?"
—*Baseball legend Satchel Paige*

"Retirement is not the end of your identity but the beginning of a new one."
– Unknown

CHAPTER 16:

Discovering Your Soul Identity, Part IV

This next section invites you to dive deep and explore the core of who you are. Soul searching can be challenging, but it's also profoundly rewarding.

1. What are you most and least confident about? Where did your insecurities come from? What has given you confidence in some areas and not in others?

2. What do you do to feel your power? Some people play loud music. Others have power poses that they do in the mirror. Some wear a certain color. What makes you feel powerful? Why?

3. Put your shoes on, go outside, and walk. Be present. Think of nothing other than what you are doing and where you are doing it. Be mindful of your breath, your heartbeat, your existence. Look at your surroundings. Whenever your mind wanders (as it undoubtedly will), just bring your focus back to your breath, then your heartbeat, then your surroundings. Just enjoy the moment, nothing more.

4. Write down every negative thought you have today. Every single one. And when you reach the end of the day, look at the list and decide how many of those thoughts were justified, and how that negativity is interfering with your happiness.

5. What are the life changes you have been most reluctant to make? What has held you back? What would it take to get you to take action?

6. How often do you follow the rules? How has this helped or hindered your life?

7. If you had to pick, what was the best year of your life? What made it so important to you? Is there a way to create that kind of good energy in your life right now? What would it take?

8. There is much to be skeptical and cynical about—if you choose to see the world through that lens. Do you? How has that affected your attitude and your life?

9. There are 168 hours in a week. Pick an average week and figure out where your time has gone. Are you spending time in alignment with your life's priorities? Are you doing what matters to your soul? How could you save some time to honor yourself?

10. Friendships can last a lifetime or flame out unexpectedly. Think for a moment about the friends who have been there for you, then look at the friendships you have lost. What are three good things and three bad that you have learned about trust and friendship over the years?

11. List the ten times you felt most alive. What were you doing that made you feel that way? What can you do to bring that energy into your daily life?

12. If a filmmaker called and said he or she wanted to do a movie on your life, what do you think the *real* story would be? Write the summary.

13. Describe a time when you felt helpless and what you did to find your way through the situation. What did you learn? How did it make you grow?

14. Have you hesitated to do what you really wanted to do because you were waiting on approval from others? How would you have lived differently if you had never worried about approval or acceptance? What if it never mattered what other people thought about you?

15. What have you settled for in life? Relationships? Bad jobs? When did you settle for less than you really wanted? Why? Are you settling now? What can you do to change things and get what you really want?

CHAPTER 17:

Doing Things Alone

I am spontaneous and generally don't know what I am doing until I am doing it.

Fortunately, I always, always, *always* have someone willing to go with me to do whatever I really want to do. That person is *me*. I am not afraid to kayak or hike or cycle or swim or shop or go to a museum or restaurant or anywhere else by myself. In fact, I often *prefer* it because I'm contemplative. I like to process what I am doing and enjoy my life.

When I go it alone, I know I am going to do what I really want to do with someone I know and love better than anyone else. I can count on myself, so I do. Admittedly, when I first started my solo ventures years ago, I took a few risks that I shouldn't have. I learned a lot in the process and try not to take unnecessary risks anymore.

If you have time on your hands and don't have anyone to join you on an adventure, learn to fly solo.

I have a lot of friends who, with few exceptions, hate camping. Because of that, I didn't camp at all for a number of years. I longed to camp out under the stars, but with no one to join me, I thought I had no choice but to give it up.

I did a lot of things alone when I was younger, and sometimes to my detriment because hiking and skiing alone into the backcountry of Colorado was not always the smartest decision. I had some close calls, and I almost got stuck out there in the wilds, and there were two times when I could easily have gotten myself killed. But by the time I was in my 40s, I was far more cautious. I would kayak alone because I was always somewhere where others could see me. But camp? No. I was convinced I would encounter a serial killer.

It ate at me. Finally, after I realized I would likely never camp again if I didn't dare go by myself, I made a reservation in a county park, got all my old camping gear together, grabbed my dog, Louie, and went. Within an hour of pitching my tent, there was a biblical thunderstorm. Louie and I sat in that tent, and I felt so hyper-alive and absolutely blessed by the universe. I felt protected and safe. Louie was fine, as long as he was with his mommy. When the storm ended, a brilliant sunset sunk into the Gulf of Mexico—and I could see it right outside my tent. I felt so blessed to be there.

After that, I started going solo regularly. I joined an outdoors club on Meetup. com, and I did enjoy camping with the group, but I never got the same joy of solitude that I experienced by myself. So, I still camped alone regularly, at least a dozen times a year. I still do.

While it might seem intimidating at first, the willingness to do things by yourself opens up the entire world to you. I sometimes joke that I'm taking myself out on a date. The company will be good, and I'll get to do whatever I want and eat wherever I want. Win-win-win. Can you try this? There is no need to coordinate schedules or compromise on activities. If you wake up one morning and decide you want to hike a new trail or explore a quaint town nearby, you can just go. This flexibility lets you dive into your interests and passions at your own pace.

If you aren't having fun, you have full control over the decision to turn around and go home. You know what that is? It is freedom!

Starting small is a great way to ease into solo activity. A day trip to a nearby town or a solo hike can be perfect initial steps. These smaller outings help you get comfortable with being your own company. As you gain experience, you'll feel your confidence growing, encouraging you to tackle bigger challenges. For instance, dining out alone or visiting a museum can be simple yet empowering experiences that build the skills needed for more significant solo adventures like dining out alone and visiting a museum *on a solo trip to Paris.*

Planning ahead can make your solo trips more enjoyable and less stressful. While spontaneity is part of the fun, having a loose itinerary can provide structure without compromising your freedom. Research your destination, including transportation options, accommodations, and local attractions. This preparation helps ensure you're well-informed and ready for your adventure. Don't forget to inform someone about your plans and check in periodically—safety should always be a priority.

One of the joys of solo adventure is that it gives you a chance to savor your solitude. Use the time for self-reflection and mindfulness because that is true soul medicine. Whether you're hiking through a quiet forest or sitting by a serene lake, the lack of distractions allows you to connect with your thoughts in nature. Embrace the opportunity to be present and appreciate the beauty around you. Solitude can be incredibly refreshing and rejuvenating.

That said, traveling alone doesn't mean you have to be lonely. Solo adventures often provide opportunities to meet interesting people along the way. Stay in hostels, join group tours, or visit local cafés and social spots to engage with fellow travelers or locals. You might make new friends or learn something new. People are often more open and approachable when you're alone, making it easier to strike up conversations and form connections.

My dear friend, Linda Brown, backpacked the world by herself for years—well into her 80s. She stayed in youth hostels and created an ever-changing tribe of nomadic travel buddies from young to old. She called them her "intergalactic friends" because she'd meet people, and it seemed like she had always known them. Linda would connect with people in hostels or while out on the road and they'd end up traveling together for a day or many days. If she didn't have people with her, she was fine. She said she always felt safe. She lived life fearlessly. Now, at 87, she's living in Mexico in assisted living. She knows her memory isn't as good as it used to be, and she knows she's not capable of doing what she used to do. But damn, she sure did it while she could. She went *everywhere*—circumnavigating the globe four times! If she'd waited for someone to do that with her, she would have gone *nowhere.* The whole world opens up to you when you are willing to do things alone. But it does take confidence.

Safety is paramount on solo trips. Trust your instincts and avoid risky situations. Stick to well-lit, populated areas, especially at night, and keep your valuables secure. If something feels off, don't hesitate to leave the area or seek help. Having a basic understanding of local customs and emergency contacts can also be beneficial.

Ultimately, solo adventures are about enjoying the experience and discovering new parts of yourself. Every step you take and every new place you visit contributes to your personal growth. Celebrate the small victories, like navigating a new city or trying a new activity. Take photos, write about your experiences, and cherish the memories you create. Learning to adventure alone is a process that can lead to profound self-discovery. Embrace the freedom, build your confidence, and enjoy yourself. With each solo adventure, you'll gain a deeper appreciation for your own company and the world around you. So pack your bag, plan your trip, and step out into the world. Your solo adventure awaits!

Affirmations for Doing It Alone

- I am strong, capable, and confident in my own company.
- I embrace the freedom and independence that comes with doing things alone.
- I trust myself to make good decisions that keep me safe.
- I love being alone because it allows me to connect with my deepest thoughts and feelings.
- I enjoy my own company and find peace and joy in solitude.
- I create some of my best memories and experiences by myself.
- I deserve to explore the world and enjoy life, whether alone or with others.
- I am brave, adventurous, and fully equipped to handle anything that comes my way.

CHAPTER 18

How Do You Want to Spend Your Retirement?

This comprehensive inventory will help you consider many options that will help you design your best retirement.

Learning and Education

16. Are you interested in taking classes or courses?

17. Do you want to learn a new language?

18. Are you interested in attending workshops or seminars?

19. Do you enjoy visiting museums or historical sites?

20. Would you consider going back to school for a degree or certification?

21. Are you interested in online learning platforms?

22. Do you enjoy attending lectures or academic talks?

23. Are you interested in joining a book club?

24. Do you enjoy watching educational documentaries?

25. Are you interested in studying philosophy or theology?

26. Do you want to learn more about history or archaeology?

27. Are you interested in studying astronomy or space science?

28. Do you enjoy learning about new technologies and innovations?

29. Are you interested in genealogy and tracing your family history?

30. Do you want to learn about investing and personal finance?

31. Are you interested in attending art or music appreciation classes?

Volunteer Work

32. Are you interested in volunteering?

33. Do you have experience with any volunteer organizations?

34. What causes are you passionate about?

35. Would you be interested in mentoring or tutoring?

36. Are you interested in participating in community service projects?

37. Do you want to volunteer at hospitals or healthcare facilities?

38. Are you interested in volunteering at schools or educational programs?

39. Do you want to help with disaster relief efforts?

40. Are you interested in environmental conservation projects?

41. Do you want to volunteer at animal shelters or wildlife rescues?

42. Are you interested in working with homeless shelters or food banks?

43. Do you want to participate in local government or civic organizations?

Interests and Hobbies

44. What are your favorite hobbies?

45. Are there any hobbies you wish to pursue in retirement?

46. Do you enjoy reading? If so, what genres?

47. Are you interested in arts and crafts? If yes, which ones?

48. Do you like gardening?

49. Are you interested in learning a musical instrument?

50. Do you enjoy cooking or baking?

51. Are you interested in photography?

52. Do you like traveling? If so, what destinations interest you?

53. Are there any sports or physical activities you enjoy?

54. Do you enjoy playing chess or other board games?

55. Are you interested in bird-watching or wildlife observation?

56. Do you enjoy fishing or hunting?

57. Are you interested in model building or collecting?

58. Do you enjoy knitting, crocheting, or sewing?

59. Are you interested in brewing your own beer or making wine?

60. Do you enjoy puzzles, like crosswords or sudoku?

61. Are you interested in calligraphy or lettering?

62. Do you enjoy woodworking or carpentry?

63. Are you interested in metalworking or welding?

Social Activities

64. Do you enjoy socializing with friends and family?

65. Are you interested in joining clubs or groups?

66. Do you enjoy attending social events or gatherings?

67. Are you interested in organizing or hosting events?

68. Would you like to participate in group travel or tours?

69. Do you enjoy playing cards or participating in game nights?

70. Are you interested in joining a community choir or music group?

71. Do you enjoy dancing or attending dance classes?

72. Are you interested in joining a sports team or league?

73. Do you want to join a fitness or yoga class with others?

74. Are you interested in participating in local theater or drama groups?

75. Do you enjoy attending cultural festivals or fairs?

Health and Wellness

76. Are you interested in maintaining or improving your physical fitness?

77. Do you follow a specific diet or nutrition plan?

78. Are you interested in yoga or meditation?

79. Do you have regular medical check-ups?

80. Are you interested in alternative health practices?

81. Do you want to participate in wellness retreats?

82. Are you interested in joining a fitness group or gym?

83. Do you practice mindfulness or stress-reduction techniques?

84. Are you interested in learning about holistic health approaches?

85. Do you have a fitness routine you follow regularly?

86. Are you interested in trying new forms of exercise?

87. Do you want to focus on mental health and emotional well-being?

88. Are you interested in attending health workshops or seminars?

Travel and Adventure

89. How often do you plan to travel?

90. Do you prefer domestic or international travel?

91. Are you interested in solo travel, group tours, or family trips?

92. Do you enjoy outdoor activities like hiking or camping?

93. Are you interested in adventurous sports?

94. Do you want to go on a cruise?

95. Are you interested in RV travel or road trips?

96. Do you enjoy visiting national parks or natural landmarks?

97. Are you interested in cultural or historical tours?

98. Do you want to explore culinary travel experiences?

99. Are you interested in eco-tourism or sustainable travel?

100. Do you enjoy visiting beaches or coastal areas?

Home and Living

101. Are you considering relocating in retirement?

102. Do you plan to downsize or move to a different type of housing?

103. Are you interested in home renovation or DIY projects?

104. Do you enjoy decorating or interior design?

105. Are you planning to create a home office or hobby space?

106. Do you want to set up a home gym or fitness area?

107. Are you interested in sustainable living practices?

108. Do you enjoy organizing and decluttering your home?

109. Are you considering living in a retirement community?

110. Do you want to create a garden or outdoor living space?

Family and Relationships

111. Do you plan to spend more time with family?

112. Are you interested in genealogy or family history research?

113. Do you have grandchildren or plan to have them soon?

114. Are you interested in caregiving for a family member?

115. Do you want to plan family reunions or gatherings?

116. Are you interested in traveling with family members?

117. Do you enjoy hosting family events or holidays?

118. Are you interested in creating family traditions or rituals?

119. Do you want to document family stories or create a family history book?

120. Are you considering moving closer to family members?

Religious and Spiritual Life

121. Do you practice a religion or follow a spiritual path?

122. Are you interested in joining a faith community or group?

123. Do you enjoy attending religious services or spiritual retreats?

124. Are you interested in exploring different spiritual practices?

125. Do you want to study religious texts or spiritual literature?

126. Are you interested in meditation or mindfulness practices?

127. Do you want to volunteer or participate in activities with your faith community?

Creativity and Self-Expression

128. Are you interested in writing, such as a blog or a book?

129. Do you enjoy painting or drawing?

130. Are you interested in learning about or practicing sculpture?

131. Do you enjoy performing arts, like theater or dance?

132. Are you interested in fashion or designing clothing?

133. Do you enjoy creating music or songwriting?

134. Are you interested in acting or taking drama classes?

135. Do you want to participate in art exhibitions or craft fairs?

136. Are you interested in creative writing workshops?

137. Do you enjoy making jewelry or other crafts?

Technology and Gadgets

138. Are you interested in learning more about technology?

139. Do you use social media?

140. Are you interested in digital photography or videography?

141. Do you enjoy playing video games or online games?

142. Are you interested in smart home technology?

143. Do you enjoy exploring new apps or software?

144. Are you interested in virtual reality or augmented reality experiences?

Community and Civic Engagement

145. Are you interested in participating in local government or community boards?

146. Do you want to be involved in neighborhood associations?

147. Are you interested in advocacy or activism?

148. Do you want to participate in environmental conservation efforts?

149. Are you interested in joining a service organization like Rotary or Lions Club?

150. Do you want to participate in local planning or development projects?

151. Are you interested in attending town hall meetings or public forums?

| WHO AM I NOW?

CHAPTER 19:

Dealing with Loneliness

"Old age ain't no place for sissies." And that is the damn truth, spoken by the legendary actress, Bette Davis. Even though she died decades ago, her words hit the mark dead-on.

That's because life gets harder the older we get. At some point, we face huge emotional challenges that come with feeling weaker, more isolated, unhealthy, and like we are losing it.

I am one of those people who wants a quick, nasty heart attack to strike me down and get me out of here, preferably before I start falling apart. I know I am not alone in that. But few of us get an easy out.

What we get is obstacle on top of obstacle on top of obstacle. There comes a point where we have to accept that it's not getting better, it's getting worse. Just thinking about that is depressing. Imagine what it's like to live with it.

Loneliness may be the worst ailment of all because we feel alone in the battle. It is hard to ward it off, too, because our loved ones are getting sick or dying, we face increased challenges with our health which impacts how we care for ourselves and how much help we need, and as all of this happens, we can experience less social interaction and an even greater loss of purpose.

That's hard on us. Sadly, loneliness itself makes matters worse, accelerating cognitive decline and Alzheimer's disease.

Sigh.

There are things you can do to fight back. First, prioritize creating new social connections, even if they aren't the ones you are used to or especially want. Every person has a story, so learn to interact and listen to people you might not ordinarily choose for friends.

My uncle was shaken when he moved into a nursing home, and I remember him telling me, "You only come to a place like this to die." But that rockstar of a human being quickly rebounded, organizing the people around him into a group of rabble-rousers who'd play cards, tell stories, and tease the staff for a few laughs. This was not his favorite moment in life, but he did not let it get swallowed by loneliness or darkness. I want to be like that.

When you feel lonely, you have to realize you are your greatest asset in dealing with this challenge. One good conversation can brighten your day, so find people to talk to and listen to. Try joining clubs or groups, even if they meet virtually. Just say yes to any possible opportunity to meet people and have a conversation.

Volunteering is such a great way to connect with others and find purpose. Helping others actually will help you. It can give you the boost you need to improve your mental health. There are plenty of places that need volunteers, like hospitals, schools, or animal shelters.

If you love animals, consider getting a pet. I've long said I can put up with just about anything as long as I've got a good dog, a cat, and streaming on a big-screen television set.

If you're feeling lonely, it might be time to find different hobbies that meet your current living and health situation. You might not be able to do the adventurous or high-octane activities you used to, but learn something new, whether it's painting, knitting, playing an instrument, or gardening. Hobbies help you fill your time in a meaningful way, and they reduce loneliness. Plus, a lot of hobbies give you a chance for social interaction with others who share your interests.

No matter what, stay physically active. It's not just good for your body—it's important for your mind. Exercise will boost your mood and energy levels and give you a better night's sleep. Join a gym, take dance classes, or do community fitness programs. If you want people to hang out with, embrace group fitness! Walking clubs, yoga, Zumba, or Pilates classes are great for social interaction.

If you still aren't getting enough social interaction, think about changing your living situation. You can move to a retirement community, which will offer social networks, activities, outings, and social events. That makes it so much easier to meet people and stay engaged.

Stay up on technology. That gets harder the longer you are out of the workplace and not constantly using it. But technology gives you so many options for staying connected to loved ones and friends you can't easily see—especially if they live far away. I frequently do virtual happy hours with friends. I network online all the time. You can do this too. No, it's not the same as being there, but it is a pretty close second. I have some close friends I haven't seen in years—but it doesn't feel that way because we see each other all the time on Zoom.

If it starts to feel overwhelming, you can join a support group or get professional help. Therapists and counselors have strategies for dealing with loneliness and can provide good support. Plus, sometimes it makes a huge difference to just verbalize what you are feeling.

There are also online communities and forums where you can meet people with similar interests.

Confronting loneliness is so similar to what you do when you design your retirement. Do the things that give you access to others, keep you busy, or stimulate your brain. Lifelong learning is a way to do all three. Many community centers, libraries, and universities offer classes for seniors, and many are free. Sign up for an online class to keep you busy during those hours at home that may seem endless. You can strengthen your mind and satisfy your curiosity at any time. Check your state's opportunities for free lifelong learning.

In Florida, where I live, higher education is free for older residents. I remember many seniors attending college with me. That's the case in most states. At this moment, four don't do it: Arizona, Idaho, Indiana, and South Dakota. Those states have significant discounts, but they aren't free. Most of these arrangements allow for auditing credit, but not degrees. Still, think of what you could learn, and think of how interesting it would be to meet other students, including younger ones, as you push yourself to learn something new.

Do something to inspire and satisfy your curiosity. The bonus is the social interaction that comes along with going to classes.

Finally, put your focus on your health. Often, loneliness is exacerbated by health issues that may ground you from your usually active life. If you are facing that, remember: There is almost always something you can do to physically challenge yourself, whether you are working out in a gym or sitting in a chair at home. This will keep you sharp and make you feel more energetic.

Loneliness is common as we age, but we can aggressively fight it. We counter it by finding social interaction, whether we can leave the house—or not. By keeping in touch with loved ones, staying active, pursuing hobbies, diving into lifelong learning, and seeking support when needed, you can combat loneliness and lead a fulfilling, connected life.

Affirmations for Dealing with Loneliness

- I am worthy of love and connection. I deserve and attract meaningful relationships.
- I attract positive and uplifting people into my life who appreciate and value me.
- I am grateful for the friendships and relationships that bring joy and companionship.
- I am always capable of reaching out and forming new connections with others.
- I know that the right people will come into my life at the right time.
- I focus on the positive things in my life, and my gratitude attracts others to me.

CHAPTER 20

Time to Get Serious About Your Bucket List

A bucket list is a collection of goals, dreams, and experiences that a person wants to achieve before they "kick the bucket" and die. The concept was popularized in the 2007 movie *The Bucket List* with Jack Nicholson and Morgan Freeman playing two terminally ill men who had some adventurous dreams they wanted to do before they kicked the bucket. They did everything from skydiving to riding motorcycles on the Great Wall of China.

What's on your list? It doesn't have to involve high-adrenaline adventure. What is your unfinished business? A bucket list often reflects a person's interests, values, and long-term dreams, giving you motivation to stay in the game and keep living.

Here are some ideas that might spike an exciting next chapter for you.

- Travel to a foreign country
- Visit all 50 states
- Learn a new language

- Write a memoir or autobiography
- Go skydiving
- Visit the Grand Canyon
- Attend a Broadway show
- Learn to play a musical instrument
- Take a road trip across the country
- Explore our national parks
- Swim with dolphins
- Go on a safari
- Ride in a hot air balloon
- Visit famous museums
- Go wine tasting in Napa Valley
- Ride a motorcycle
- Attend a major sports event (e.g., Super Bowl, World Series)
- Spend a month at the beach
- Learn to sail
- Visit the pyramids in Egypt
- Go scuba diving
- Participate in a marathon or 5K
- Learn to dance (salsa, tango, etc.)
- Take a European river cruise
- See the Northern Lights
- Write a novel or some short stories
- Visit the Great Wall of China
- Go whale watching
- Attend a famous music festival
- Visit the Eiffel Tower
- Go to a spa retreat
- Visit Machu Picchu

- Go fishing in Alaska
- Take a train trip
- Explore ancient ruins
- Go zip-lining
- Visit a castle in Europe
- Go bird-watching
- Visit Japan during cherry blossom season
- Go on a pilgrimage (e.g., Camino de Santiago)
- Visit all the continents
- Visit historic battlefields
- Go on a silent retreat
- Visit Australia and New Zealand
- Go to the Kentucky Derby
- Take a helicopter ride
- Explore the Galápagos Islands
- Visit Hawaii
- Take a culinary tour
- Go snorkeling in the Great Barrier Reef
- Visit Venice and ride a gondola
- Explore Antarctica
- Take a cruise to Alaska
- Go to a famous jazz festival
- Visit the Vatican
- Take a trip to the Amazon rainforest
- Learn to brew beer
- Visit Icelands Blue Lagoon
- See a Broadway musical
- Learn to surf
- Visit the Louvre Museum

- Go to a fashion show
- Go on a road trip in an RV
- Visit the Amazon River
- Learn to fly a plane
- Visit the Smithsonian Museums
- Hike on the Appalachian Trail
- Visit Canadas national parks
- Take a cruise through the Panama Canal
- Visit the Taj Mahal
- Climb a lighthouse
- Visit a monastery
- Take a meditation retreat
- Visit a planetarium
- Go on a camping trip
- Visit a castle
- Go to a historical reenactment
- Go to an opera performance
- Go to a lantern festival
- Visit a famous restaurant
- Take a bird-watching tour
- Visit a famous cemetery
- Go to a classical music festival
- Take a cooking class abroad
- Visit an archaeological site

Now that you have some ideas, let's take a look at your unfinished business. What do you *really* want to do to make this time in your life the best it can possibly be?

1. What places in the world have you always dreamed of visiting?

2. What new skills or hobbies would you like to learn or master?

3. Are there any adventure activities, like skydiving, zip-lining, or scuba diving, that you want to experience?

4. Which historical or cultural sites do you want to see?

5. What personal achievements, such as writing a book or running a marathon, do you aspire to accomplish?

6. Are there any significant life events, like a family reunion or a milestone celebration, you want to organize or attend?

7. Are there any sports events, concerts, or festivals you want to attend?

8. Do you have any educational goals, like taking a class or earning a degree in a new field?

9. What unique experiences, such as riding in a hot air balloon or taking a train trip, appeal to you?

10. Which natural wonders, like the Grand Canyon or the northern lights, do you want to see?

11. Are there any creative projects, like painting or crafting, that you'd like to pursue?

12. Are there any health or fitness goals, such as practicing yoga regularly or completing a triathlon, that you want to achieve?

Now, start your list. Are you ready to commit and actually live your dreams? You know you aren't going to live forever and the time for delaying things has passed. Are you ready and willing to figure out, schedule, and have the experiences that will bring you the most joy and fulfillment? Write down your aspirations without limiting yourself, allowing your imagination to run free. Prioritize the items that resonate most deeply with you, and visualize yourself achieving them. This initial step of clearly defining your dreams sets the foundation for turning them into reality.

Once you have a well-defined bucket list, break down each goal into actionable steps. This makes seemingly daunting dreams more manageable and doable. For example, if one of your goals is to travel to a specific country, research the destination, set your budget, and plan your itinerary. It's less overwhelming if you break the process into smaller tasks, such as booking flights, securing accommodations, and learning basic phrases in the local language. By creating a detailed plan, you turn abstract dreams into concrete actions.

Make this a priority and schedule time to work on planning and achieving your wildest dreams. It's easy to let daily routines and responsibilities take over, but consciously set aside time to work on this so you actually do it. Whether it's dedicating a weekend each month to exploring new places or setting aside an hour each day to practice a new skill, consistent effort is key.

This may push you out of your comfort zone. Welcome that! That is how you grow and fill your life with living. Many of the most rewarding experiences involve a degree of risk or challenge. Don't be afraid to try new things, meet new people, or travel to unfamiliar places. The discomfort you may feel initially will be outweighed by the satisfaction and joy of achieving something meaningful.

Finally, share this journey with others. Whether it's friends, family, or a community of like-minded individuals, sharing your goals and progress can provide motivation, encouragement, and accountability. That helps you move forward and inspires them to do the same in their own lives.

This bucket list business isn't about checking things off. It's about the whole process. Enjoy every step of the experience. Your time at the top of the mountain is short, but the climb is long and magnificent.

CHAPTER 21:

Health Matters

Taking care of your health in retirement is incredibly important, and if you've backburnered it until now, it's not too late to forgive yourself and start making some changes. My neighbor retired, excited to finally have time to relax and enjoy life without the stress of work. But within a few months, he started feeling sluggish and unwell. He woke up in the middle of the night feeling like his chest was being squeezed. His breath was short, and he was lightheaded and completely exhausted. He called 911.

It was a mild heart attack. A big, noticeable warning sign that he needed to stop neglecting his health and start taking responsibility for it because, at this point in life, we are all fighting for our lives.

It's hard to enjoy retirement if you're not feeling your best. This is why taking a proactive approach to your health is so important. When you're retired, you have more control over your schedule, which means more opportunities to incorporate healthy habits into your daily routine.

Regular physical activity can help maintain your mobility, strength, balance, and overall health. Whether it's taking a daily walk, joining a fitness class, or even gardening, keeping your body moving helps keep your mind sharp and your spirits high.

My neighbor started going for morning walks, and it made a world of difference. He felt more energetic and happier, and it gave him a sense of purpose each day.

Eating well is another key aspect. It's easy to slip into habits of convenience foods and snacks, but taking the time to prepare nutritious meals can do wonders for your health. Fresh fruits, vegetables, whole grains, and lean proteins should be staples in your diet. These foods provide the nutrients your body needs to stay strong and fight off illnesses. My neighbor began experimenting with new recipes and found a new passion for cooking, which not only improved his health but also gave him a fun and creative outlet.

Don't forget about mental health. Retirement can sometimes lead to feelings of loneliness or a lack of purpose, which can affect your mental well-being. Staying connected with friends and family, pursuing hobbies, and even volunteering can keep your mind engaged and your heart fulfilled. My neighbor started volunteering at a local animal shelter, which gave him a sense of community and joy. It's these little things that make a big difference.

Last, regular check-ups with your doctor are essential. Preventive care can catch potential health issues before they become serious. You want a good life? Be proactive rather than reactive when it comes to your health.

Retirement is a wonderful chapter in your life's story, but to fully enjoy it, you have to prioritize your health. By staying active, eating well, nurturing your mental health, and keeping up with medical appointments, you're setting yourself up for a happier, healthier, and more fulfilling time. My neighbor's journey shows that it's never too late to start taking care of yourself, and the benefits will fill your life with life.

The Top 5 Things to Do to Take Care of Your Body

I have been a fitness nut since my late 20s. Before that, I didn't work out at all. The greatest tip I have is this: Make a promise to yourself that every morning—no matter what—you will put your shoes on and walk to the end of the driveway. You can give yourself permission to turn around and go back home, and even go right back to bed. But you must, must, *must* first get down the driveway. I made that commitment when I was 25 years old and have kept it almost every day since. Once I get to the street, I figure I might as well go for a walk. It isn't going to kill me. Actually, it's going to help keep me alive.

One thing that has made it easy is that I've got a big dog. He's got to be walked, so there's not much debate about getting up and going. But I'd do it either way. It's a promise I made to myself, and keeping that promise has given me a foundation of health and happiness as I start every day.

1. Stay Physically Active

Regular exercise is essential for maintaining mobility, strength, and overall health. Activities such as walking, swimming, yoga, and strength training can help:

- Improve cardiovascular health
- Enhance muscle and bone strength
- Boost mood and energy levels
- Reduce the risk of chronic diseases

2. Eat a Balanced Diet

A nutritious diet supports overall health and helps prevent various age-related issues. Focus on:

- Eating plenty of fruits and vegetables
- Choosing whole grains over refined grains
- Including lean proteins such as fish, chicken, and plant-based options

- Limiting sugar, salt, and unhealthy fats
- Staying hydrated

3. Regular Health Check-Ups

Preventive care is crucial for early detection and management of health conditions. Regular check-ups with your healthcare provider can help:

- Monitor chronic conditions like hypertension and diabetes
- Update vaccinations and screenings
- Adjust medications as needed
- Discuss any new symptoms or health concerns

4. Stay Socially Engaged

Maintaining social connections is important for mental and emotional well-being. So many studies show that your social network keeps your mind in the game and helps ward off dementia and Alzheimer's disease. Activities to stay socially engaged include:

- Participating in community groups or clubs
- Volunteering
- Keeping in touch with friends and family
- Joining fitness classes or hobby groups

5. Prioritize Mental Health

Mental health is just as important as physical health. To support mental well-being:

- Practice mindfulness or meditation
- Engage in cognitive activities like puzzles, reading, or learning new skills
- Get enough sleep
- Seek help if experiencing feelings of depression, anxiety, or loneliness

Great Physical Activity for Seniors

By focusing on these key areas, older adults can enhance their quality of life, maintain independence, and enjoy their retirement years more fully.

Walking

Benefits: Low-impact, improves cardiovascular health, strengthens muscles, and enhances mood.

Tips: Aim for at least 30 minutes a day and consider varying the pace to include brisk walking.

Swimming and Water Aerobics

Benefits: Gentle on the joints, excellent for cardiovascular health, improves flexibility, and strengthens muscles.

Tips: Join a class to stay motivated and ensure proper technique.

Tai Chi

Benefits: Enhances balance, flexibility, and strength; reduces stress and improves mental well-being.

Tips: Start with a beginner class to learn the basic movements and gradually progress.

Yoga

Benefits: Improves flexibility, balance, and strength; promotes relaxation and mental clarity.

Tips: Choose classes or routines designed for seniors, focusing on gentle and restorative yoga.

Strength Training

Benefits: Increases muscle mass and bone density, improves metabolism, and enhances overall strength.

Tips: Use light weights, resistance bands, or body-weight exercises; aim for two to three sessions per week.

Cycling

Benefits: Low-impact, great for cardiovascular health, strengthens leg muscles.

Tips: Consider stationary bikes for safety and convenience, especially in inclement weather.

Dancing

Benefits: Improves cardiovascular health, enhances coordination and balance, boosts mood.

Tips: Join a dance class like ballroom, line dancing, or Zumba Gold, which is tailored for older adults.

Pilates

Benefits: Strengthens core muscles, improves posture, and enhances flexibility.

Tips: Look for Pilates classes designed for seniors or those with low-impact modifications.

Stretching

Benefits: Maintains flexibility, reduces stiffness, and improves range of motion.

Tips: Incorporate daily stretching routines, focusing on all major muscle groups.

Gardening

Benefits: Combines light physical activity with mental relaxation, promotes flexibility and strength.

Tips: Use ergonomic tools to reduce strain and take frequent breaks to avoid overexertion.

Safety Tips for Exercising

Consult Your Doctor: Before starting any new exercise regimen, it's important to discuss it with your healthcare provider, especially if you have chronic conditions or mobility issues.

Warm-Up and Cool-Down: Always start with a gentle warm-up to prepare your muscles and end with a cool-down to prevent stiffness.

Stay Hydrated: Drink plenty of water before, during, and after exercise.

Listen to Your Body: Pay attention to any discomfort or pain, and modify exercises as needed to avoid injury.

Incorporating physical activities into your routine can significantly enhance your physical and mental well-being, helping you enjoy a healthier, more active retirement.

CHAPTER 22

Getting Motivated

Starting a workout routine can seem overwhelming, especially if you don't like exercise or have never really done it. It's not too late. Actually, it's never too late to embrace a healthier lifestyle, and the benefits are life-changing whether you are 40 or 80. The key to finding motivation is understanding the impact exercise can have on your life.

How can you motivate yourself?

Regular exercise isn't just about getting in shape; it's about improving the way you feel. It is about your overall health, not just your muscles. The right program can help manage chronic heart disease, diabetes, and arthritis. It strengthens your muscles, improves your balance, and reduces the risk of falls. Just imagine how wonderful it would feel to move more freely, maintain your independence, and have fewer aches and pains. Knowing that each step you take is a step toward a healthier future can be incredibly motivating.

Exercise kept me from falling into a black hole after my long-ago divorce. Seeing how well it worked, it became a critical, go-to component for maintaining my mental health in the decades since. I have a coping strategy that involves God, exercise, fresh air, affirmations, and gratitude. Exercise is an all-natural remedy for depression, and combined with healthy eating and other good lifestyle choices, it can make you quite happy. You can't really understand how good it makes you feel until you actually make some changes and feel it.

Physical activity releases endorphins, the "feel-good" hormones that boost your mood and help reduce feelings of anxiety and depression. It also keeps your mind sharp and improves cognitive function. It makes you more energetic, mentally alert, and emotionally balanced. Exercise is a natural way to lift your spirits and keep your brain active, which is so important at this point.

You don't have to run a marathon the first week. Start small with activities you enjoy, like walking, stretching, or light yoga. Setting small, achievable goals and gradually increasing your activity level helps you avoid burnout and injury. Celebrate each milestone, even if you think it is no big deal. Every step forward is progress and deserves recognition.

Social support can make a huge difference in staying motivated. Join a local fitness class, and if you feel more comfortable attending classes with seniors, do that. You've got a ton of options, like water aerobics, tai chi, or dancing. Exercising with others can make the experience more enjoyable and give you a sense of community. Plus, having a workout buddy or joining a group adds a level of accountability that makes you more likely to stick with your new routine. Turning exercise into a social activity makes it seem less of a chore.

Variety is key to keeping things interesting. Mix up your routine to keep it engaging. Work different muscle groups. Try incorporating strength training, balance exercises, and cardio into your schedule. This variety not only keeps things exciting but also ensures a well-rounded approach to fitness. You might swim on Monday, do yoga on Tuesday, lift weights on Wednesday, or whatever. You'll find that different activities can be enjoyable and keep you looking forward to your workouts.

Listen to your body. Push yourself, but also know your limits. If something doesn't feel right, adjust your activity level or take a rest day. The goal is long-term health and enjoyment, not short-term gains or unnecessary pain. Over time, you'll learn what works best for you and how to balance exertion with recovery. This mindful approach helps maintain a positive relationship with exercise, ensuring you stay motivated and injury-free.

Think about the future you want for yourself—more energy to enjoy your play with your family, the strength to travel, or simply the ability to live independently. Keeping these personal goals in mind can be a powerful source of motivation.

All you have to do is get started.

Affirmations for Exercise

- I am strong, capable, and committed to doing this to improve my health.
- Every step I take brings me closer to my fitness goals.
- This makes me feel vibrant, energetic, and healthy.
- I enjoy moving my body and feeling it grow stronger each day.
- I am patient with myself and trust the process of becoming more fit.
- I prioritize my health every day.

CHAPTER 23:

Financial Insecurities

Retirement should be a time of relaxation and enjoyment, but for many, financial insecurity can cast a shadow over this phase of life. It's natural to worry about whether your savings will last, how you'll handle unexpected expenses, or what changes you might need to make to maintain your lifestyle. While these concerns are valid, there are ways to deal with your financial insecurity and find a sense of stability and peace of mind. Freaking yourself out and worrying excessively accomplishes nothing.

There is no way that a short chapter in a workbook will define and solve your financial concerns—especially if I'm writing it. But I can point you in the right direction. My most important piece of advice here is to confront the issue. Don't passively wait for things to resolve themselves. Do something.

Take stock of your current financial situation. This means listing all your sources of income, such as pensions, Social Security benefits, investments, and any part-time work. At the same time, compile a detailed record of your expenses. Understanding where your money is coming from and where it's going is the foundation of financial planning. If you haven't done this already, now is the perfect time.

Once you have a clear picture, consider creating a budget. A well-planned budget can help you prioritize essential expenses and identify areas where you can cut back. Remember, budgeting isn't about restricting your enjoyment but rather ensuring you have enough to cover your needs and some of your wants. It's about making informed decisions that align with your financial reality.

Exploring ways to reduce expenses can also be beneficial. This might mean downsizing your home, taking advantage of senior discounts, or finding more cost-effective ways to enjoy hobbies and social activities. Sometimes, small adjustments can lead to significant savings over time.

Don't hesitate to seek professional advice. Financial advisers can provide valuable insights and help you make decisions that align with your long-term goals. They can assist in restructuring your investments to generate more stable income or help with tax planning to maximize your savings. Most financial service companies have computerized do-it-yourself financial planning options that cost nothing and are supported by advisers who can give you phone help.

Additionally, consider the potential benefits of part-time or freelance work. Many retirees find that working part-time not only supplements their income but also provides a sense of purpose and social engagement. Whether it's consulting in your previous field, tutoring, or turning a hobby into a small business, there are many ways to earn extra money while enjoying retirement.

Remember, financial security in retirement isn't just about money—it's also about peace of mind. Focus on maintaining a healthy and active lifestyle, which can reduce healthcare costs and enhance your overall well-being. Stay connected with friends and family, and don't be afraid to discuss your concerns with them. Emotional support can make a big difference in how you handle financial stress.

Finally, be kind to yourself. It's easy to feel anxious about the future, but take things one step at a time. Celebrate small victories, like sticking to your budget for a month or finding a new source of income. Retirement is a journey, and while financial challenges may arise, with careful planning, resourcefulness, and a positive mindset, you can navigate these uncertainties and enjoy the richness of this new phase of life.

Affirmations for Financial Security

- I am capable of managing my finances wisely and confidently.
- My worry is in check because my financial situation is improving with each positive step I take.
- I have the power to adjust my spending to align with my current needs.
- I am resourceful and find creative solutions to financial challenges.
- I am becoming more financially secure and stable every day.
- I am grateful for the resources and support available to me.
- I deserve to enjoy retirement without constant financial worry.
- I enjoy my retirement without constant financial worry.

"Anyone who stops learning is old, whether at 20 or 80. Anyone who keeps learning stays young."
—Henry Ford

"Old age is always 15 years older than I am."
—Oliver Wendell Holmes

"You are only young once, but you can stay immature indefinitely."
— Poet Ogden Nash

"We are always the same age inside."
— Gertrude Stein

CHAPTER 24:

Volunteering

*"The best way to find yourself is to lose
yourself in the service of others."*
—Mahatma Gandhi

*"Remember that the happiest people are
not those getting more, but those giving more."*
— H. Jackson Brown Jr.

*"You make a living by what you get.
You make a life by what you give."*
— Winston Churchill

So, there you have it. If you want to feel better about yourself, give a little of yourself.

"The most valuable thing you have to give is your time," my high school teacher said.

He was so right. Instead of making a contribution to an organization, give an hour and get contributions from ten people. Or teach someone to read. Or just listen to somebody. Your time is valuable, and when you give it away to help others, you feel its worth.

Every time I help others, it feels like they have helped me.

Volunteering helps fulfill the sense of purpose you may have lost when you stopped working. Showing up for a volunteer job can give you some of the sense of structure and responsibility that you used to have, and the bonus payoff is you are helping advance people, a cause, or an organization that needs you.

You have valuable skill sets that you spent a lifetime accumulating. Volunteering can give you an opportunity to use those skills. In the process, you'll gain new, current skills that will stimulate your brain. This keeps you active and challenged. It can push you physically and mentally, and it can combat feelings of isolation or depression. You are giving to your community, but your community is giving to you.

This puts you in contact with other people, and that helps satisfy your human need for social connection. You will meet people who have similar interests and values, and that fosters friendships and a sense of community.

Organizations are thrilled to get reliable volunteers who are willing to show up on time and pitch in. That gives you routine and structure, plus a sense of accomplishment. It gives these organizations one thing they desperately need but can't afford: help. What a great way to stay engaged in your community and find meaning and fulfillment. Helping others will make you feel better about yourself.

The big question is deciding who you want to help. You may want to try several organizations before you decide which one is the best fit for you. Do not feel guilty telling an organization you aren't right for them. This is about you committing to an organization that will bring out your best so you can deliver your best right back.

I can't give you a list of all the organizations in your area, but I can give you some places to look. Here's a general roadmap to great volunteer opportunities: Local Nonprofits and Community Centers: Check out organizations like food banks, homeless shelters, youth centers, senior centers, and community gardens.

Environmental Organizations: Look for local chapters of national or international environmental organizations focused on conservation, clean-ups, or sustainability projects. Check out the Sierra Club or Audubon Society.

Animal Shelters and Rescues: Many shelters and animal rescues rely heavily on volunteers for animal care, adoption events, and fundraising.

Hospitals and Nursing Homes: Volunteer opportunities in healthcare settings can include assisting patients, supporting families, or administrative tasks.

Libraries and Museums: These often need volunteers for events, workshops, daily tasks, and educational programs.

Crisis Hotlines and Support Services: Suicide prevention hotlines, domestic violence shelters, drug abuse programs, mental health services, guardian ad litem, and other social service programs are often desperate for volunteers trained in counseling or support roles.

Arts and Cultural Organizations: Local theaters, art galleries, music festivals, or cultural events will be thrilled for your help.

Schools and Educational Programs: Volunteer at local schools, tutoring programs, literacy initiatives, or afterschool programs.

Sports and Recreation Centers: Volunteer for coaching youth sports teams, organizing events, or maintaining facilities.

Faith-Based Organizations: Churches, synagogues, mosques, and other religious institutions often have volunteer programs that serve the community in various ways.

General Service Organizations: Rotary has community service projects, international humanitarian efforts, youth leadership programs, and fundraising events. This goes on and on with service groups like Kiwanis International, Lions Club, and the Optimist Club.

Specialized Volunteer Opportunities: How about Habitat for Humanity, where you can help build or renovate homes, help in their ReStore retail outlet, or in advocacy? Or the American Red Cross, where you help with disaster response, blood donation drives, health and safety training, or support for military families? Perhaps you want to help Big Brothers Big Sisters, Meals on Wheels, Boy Scouts and Girl Scouts, Boys and Girls Clubs, Special Olympics, the American Cancer Society, Salvation Army, or a million other groups.

Being a great volunteer involves more than just showing up; it requires dedication, empathy, and a commitment to making a positive impact.

Organizations depend on volunteers to be consistent and reliable. That means showing up on time, honoring commitments, and communicating effectively if there are issues or changes to availability.

Your ability to show empathy and respect toward the people you are serving and your fellow volunteers is crucial. Volunteers often work with people who are vulnerable or desperate. Approach every interaction with kindness and respect for their dignity and privacy.

There may be times when you give and give and give and may not feel appreciated. The organization may not have the best leadership or most appreciative clients in the world, but you matter. Always focus on the people you are helping and what you know you are contributing—even if it sometimes feels thankless.

Great communication skills are essential for effective volunteering. Actively listen to instructions and feedback, ask questions when needed, and communicate clearly with other volunteers and staff members.

You may feel you know ten times as much as your supervisor or the executive director. You probably do. You may be volunteering for a great leader or an incompetent jerk. Many of these people are doing the best they can with limited resources. They are tasked with solving huge problems but often lack the resources to do their jobs.

Even if they don't make you feel valued, you are gold.

CHAPTER 25:

Where Are You Going to Live?

Is it time to get moving?

As we leave the workforce, moves are often inevitable. Some people need to downsize as a matter of cost. Some want a better climate. Others want to be near family. Some don't want to deal with maintenance. There are those who are seeking lower taxes. There are so many reasons to move at this juncture. Nearly half of the people who sell their homes after 65 are downsizing. Forty percent of older working people plan to move to a different city after they retire. One in four retirees move soon after they stop working.

Are you going to stay put or move on? This question is about lifestyle and personality as well as practicality and finances. Fortunately, you've got a lot of choices.

People are getting very creative about the communities they want to enjoy as they age. Choices that were once easy or obvious are less practical because of changing costs. For example, mobile home parks in Florida were a great fallback answer for so many retirees. As hurricanes grew stronger and insurance premiums and lot rents skyrocketed, mobile home life stopped being the inexpensive Plan B. Lot rents are often as high as a mortgage payment. The same goes for condominiums, because HOA fees have shot up because of the Florida insurance nightmare. Plus, assessments can be outrageous because of new laws enacted after the condo collapse in Surfside. I just had lunch with friends who live in a popular waterfront complex nearby who are facing an assessment this year for $125,000! The association expects that many of those units are going to be foreclosed upon because the senior citizens who own them cannot afford their assessments.

Here are some of your options:

1. The Standard:
- House
- Condominium
- Mobile Home
- Apartment

2. Retirement Communities:
- These are planned communities specifically designed for older adults.
- They often offer amenities like fitness centers, social activities, and sometimes healthcare services.
- Some communities are virtual cities for people over 55 with endless things to do, social opportunities, and recreation.
- These also may include independent living, assisted living, and nursing care, allowing residents to transition between levels of care as needed.

3. Cluster Living:

- Also known as co-housing, this model involves small communities where residents have their own private homes but share common spaces and activities.
- It promotes social interaction and a sense of community while allowing for independence.

4. Independent Living:

- Independent living communities cater to active seniors who do not require assistance with daily activities.
- These communities typically offer maintenance-free housing, social activities, and sometimes amenities like dining options and transportation services.

5. Assisted Living:

- Assisted living facilities provide housing and supportive services to seniors who need help with the activities of daily living such as bathing, dressing, and medication management.
- They offer a balance of independence and support, with staff available around the clock to assist residents as needed.

6. Creative Community Initiatives:

- **Village Model:** Seniors organize themselves into communities to support aging in place. They coordinate services like transportation, home repairs, and social activities.
- **Intergenerational Housing:** Programs where seniors live with younger adults or families, fostering mutual support and companionship.
- **Shared Housing:** Seniors share a home or apartment to reduce costs and provide companionship.

- **Home Modifications and Aging in Place:** You can always stay put. Many seniors choose to modify their existing homes to accommodate aging needs, including installing ramps, grab bars, and other accessibility features.

These housing options cater to varying levels of independence and care needs. You should choose an environment that best suits your preferences, health, and social needs —not just now, but also as you age.

Rent or Own?

Rent? Own? It depends. Here are some considerations to help guide your decision:

Renting in Retirement:

1. **Flexibility:** Renting provides flexibility, as it allows you to move more easily if your circumstances or preferences change. This can be advantageous if you anticipate relocating or downsizing because it allows you to make changes quickly, without the commitment or hassle of selling a home.

2. **Lower Upfront Costs:** Renting typically requires lower upfront costs compared to purchasing a home.

3. **Predictable Expenses:** Monthly expenses are predictable, as maintenance and repairs are generally the responsibility of the landlord. This can help with budgeting and financial planning in retirement.

4. **No Property Taxes or Insurance:** Renters are generally not responsible for property taxes or homeowner's insurance, which can reduce overall housing costs.

5. **Avoiding Maintenance:** Renting means you won't have to worry about the costs or physical demands of maintaining a property, something that can be particularly appealing as you age.

Owning in Retirement:

1. **Building Equity:** Homeownership allows you to build equity over time, potentially providing a valuable asset or source of funds through a reverse mortgage or sale later in retirement.

2. **Stability and Control:** Owning your home provides stability and control over your living environment, allowing you to personalize and modify the space to suit your needs and preferences.

3. **Potential Investment:** Real estate can appreciate over time, providing potential financial benefits. This can be important if you view homeownership as part of your long-term financial strategy or legacy planning.

4. **Tax Benefits:** Homeowners may benefit from tax deductions on mortgage interest and property taxes, potentially reducing taxable income.

5. **Long-Term Cost Control:** While initial costs can be higher, owning a home means your housing costs (e.g., mortgage payments) may remain more stable over time compared to rental prices, which can increase with market conditions.

Factors to Consider:

- **Financial Readiness:** Assess your financial situation, including retirement savings, income sources, and ability to afford homeownership costs like mortgage, property taxes, and maintenance.

- **Lifestyle Preferences:** Consider your desired level of stability, flexibility, and whether you prefer to handle homeownership responsibilities or prefer the convenience of renting.

- **Market Conditions:** Evaluate current real estate market trends and rental prices in your desired location, as well as potential appreciation or depreciation of property values.

- **Health and Aging Considerations:** Think about your health status and future needs for accessibility and care. Certain housing options may better accommodate aging in place or access to medical facilities.

Ultimately, this comes down to you. What do you want? Weigh the pros and cons carefully, consult with financial advisers or real estate professionals, and then do what is best for you as an individual.

Should I Stay or Should I Go Now?

Here are questions to help you clarify what you want to do about your living situation.

1. Current Situation:
- What is your current living situation (e.g., own a house, rent an apartment, live with family)?
- How satisfied are you with your current housing arrangement?

2. Location Preferences:
- Do you prefer to live in the same area/community you currently reside in, or are you open to relocating?
- What specific locations have you thought about relocating to?

3. Type of Housing:
- Would you prefer to continue living in your house, downsize to a smaller house, or consider an apartment or condominium?
- Are there specific features (e.g., single-story, proximity to amenities, outdoor space) that are important to you?

4. Community and Social Life:
- How important is it for you to be part of a community or have social interactions with neighbors?
- Would you prefer a retirement community with organized activities and amenities? What do you need?

5. Financial Considerations:

- What is your budget for housing expenses (mortgage/rent, utilities, maintenance)?
- Have you considered any financial benefits or implications of downsizing or moving to a different location?

6. Health and Accessibility:

- Do you have any current or anticipated health considerations that might influence your housing choice (e.g., accessibility features, proximity to medical facilities)?
- How important is it for you to have services and amenities that cater to older adults? What do you need?

7. Lifestyle Preferences:

- Are there specific hobbies or interests you would like your housing arrangement to accommodate, like fitness facilities, golf, gardening, or proximity to cultural activities?
- Do you prefer a quieter environment or one with more activity and social opportunities?

8. Family and Visitors:

- How often do you expect to have family or friends visit you in your new home?
- Would you prefer accommodations that allow for guests to stay comfortably?

9. Long-Term Planning:

- How do you envision your housing needs evolving over the next five to ten years?

- Have you considered factors such as aging in place, resale value of the property, or estate planning?

Personal Preferences and Priorities:
- What are your top three priorities when it comes to choosing a new housing arrangement?
- Is there anything else not covered that you feel is important to consider in helping you find the ideal housing?

Getting into the Moving Mindset

For some people, moving is the easiest thing in the world. Some people have moved dozens of times in their lives, and one more move is just one more move. But for others, it seems like an impossible challenge. They may have decades worth of clutter and don't know where to begin. Should they toss, donate, or pack it? Downsizing can be daunting and, really, who actually *likes* the process of moving? I've never had a good move. They've all had their problems. But I always remind myself that the pain was always short-lived. I deal with it, lean into it, and get it done. Then I get to be in a whole new, wonderful place.

I made sure the house I'm living in now was move-in ready when I bought it. Boy, did I get sold a bag of goods. The inspector missed huge, expensive problems. The prior owner took out all the appliances that had been in the house when I saw it and replaced them with garbage from Craigslist. It took months and cost a fortune to get this place in shape for me to move in. I was finally able to move in at the exact time my father was dying. My mother had died just two months earlier, and I knew that, in the fog of my grief, it would be a very long time before I felt up to unpacking and getting settled. Wisely, I sent out a call for help to my friends. Ten of them showed up and unpacked my kitchen, my bathrooms, my guest rooms, and my bedroom. That left me with just my office and about ten other boxes. By the time I went to bed that night, I was pretty much settled in my home. I got to my dad's bedside the next morning. Sadly, he passed two days later. The next morning, back in my new home, the plumbing backed up and there was a horrific mess. Sludge in my new dining room. But you know what? I got through it. Other moves were also challenging. Once, thousands of dollars' worth of fragile items arrived, broken. Another time—a corporate cross-country move—the movers packed everything for us. *Everything.* That included our garbage! It was left in the truck, closed up with our stuff for almost two weeks.

No, moving is not fun. But, in every case, everything worked out. There were temporary moments of chaos, followed by an adjustment, followed by good times. I believe it's up to us to choose to be happy wherever we are. That's the big part of this. My rule for moving? Suck it up, get on with things, just be happy.

I know someone who has moved to a different state almost every year since he got out of college. He's now in his 70s and it's harder for him to get jobs, so he's settling down. But he was always searching for the place where he could be happy. It's a very powerful thing to know that I can find happiness just about anywhere. I don't think I would be happy if I were in prison or surrounded with any kind of zealot, but for the most part, every place I have lived has been a happy place.

If you can choose that for your future, change will be powerful for you. Some of the changes that come later in our lives, whether we wind up in assisted living or, heaven help us, skilled nursing care, won't be our first choice for how we want to live. And I'm not sure I'm up to any of that, having watched what my mother experienced when she was in a nursing home for seven years. But I do know that wherever I go, I will be the organizer, the leader, the badass who finds and creates fun with the people around me. I know I'll do everything I can to have the best attitude I can.

The decision to move often has unsettling financial considerations. Many of us wonder if we have enough money to survive as long as we might live. Some of us have more than enough, and some have very little. Our future housing can involve agonizing decisions. Don't talk only to your financial advisor. At this point in life, we all need a cabinet of advisors who can help us to make good decisions as we move forward. Include your best friends, but also check in with people who, professionally, may have been lawyers, accountants, and realtors.

And, of course, when you move, you have to make new friends, which can be a great new opportunity or not so great. Especially if you are going from a house where you have maximum privacy to a community where you may have people living on top of or right next to you. Be very deliberate as you interact. Sometimes, it's all sunshine and happiness. But there will be a share of your new neighbors who might be nosey, grouchy, mentally ill, or outright jerks. Give yourself time and space to find your tribe. And find friends who *don't* live in the community, too. If you miss your old neighbors, go visit or have a virtual glass of wine or beer together. Often, the first people you meet are the people who need friends the most. It may be that they are new, or it may be that other people don't like them for a reason.

In general, mind your own business. There are a lot of agendas at play in any community. See what's going on. Don't choose sides. Some of these places are driven by negativity and gossip, but if you stay to the side, you are insulated from all of it. Be very pleasant when you move there but be very selective about with whom and how you interact. Don't share your personal business. Take some time to figure out what's going on. You may be lucky and wind up in a place filled with wonderful new friends. Study the landscape and find your people.

Also, wait a good while before you judge whether you like a place or not. A friend told me long ago never to judge a place until I had lived there a year. That became my standard. But as I age, I see that sometimes it takes a little longer than that. People can be slower to befriend you. Just assume you are going to be in for a bit of a wild ride at first, but it will all come together in time when you get settled and find new friends.

CHAPTER 26

Declutter Basics—Because We Need To

It doesn't matter whether you stay or go: At this point in life, it's time to get rid of your clutter.

Every time I get a load of stuff out of my house, I feel lighter. It's freeing and liberating. The energy in my home shifts. As someone who sometimes lives in a camping van for months at a time, I am always amazed how that sixty square foot van contains every single thing I need. If it doesn't, I can go to a store. I have to wonder why I have a big home full of stuff when I do so well in a little van. I live alone. I don't need this much house, and I know a move is in front of me. My only question is, what kind of move?

As I ponder that, I also ponder my clutter.

I am a big fan of The FlyLady, Marla Ciley, who has the simplest decluttering strategies anywhere. She is my guru because her books are so easy to incorporate into my life. I used to travel so much for my work, and I'd come home to a growing pile of mail on my dining room table that I just couldn't deal with. It got bigger and bigger, and it stressed me out every time I looked at it.

That is a "hot spot" according to The FlyLady. Getting rid of it meant setting a timer for 15 minutes and just giving it 15 minutes. The first time I vowed to try this technique, I delayed that 15 minutes of work all day. I finally told myself, "It's just 15 minutes." I set the timer, and when the 15 minutes was over, I was almost done clearing that hot spot! If I would hang in there 15 more minutes, there would be no pile of mail. That energy of mess and unfinished business would be out of my life!

The FlyLady taught me about the "27-Fling Boogie," which means racing through a cluttered area and tossing, donating, or relocating 27 things that don't belong there. It's an arbitrary number, but what a fast way to clear out clutter.

And while Marie Kondo got famous and made a fortune telling people to declutter by asking if each thing brings "joy," The FlyLady was talking about that decades earlier. She has always said to ask yourself, "Do I love it? Do I need it? Do I use it?" If the answer is no to all three, The FlyLady says it is clutter.

She also emphasized the value of doing a little every day rather than everything all at once, which is overwhelming. So do a little, find the hot spots and do a "hot spot fire drill," and regularly do something to keep yourself in check. Set Up "Zone Cleaning." Divide your home into zones (usually five) and focus on decluttering and deep cleaning one zone each week. This method ensures that every part of your home gets regular attention. Consistency is what creates a clutter-free environment.

I have one other trick. I look at all of the decorations and treasures I've gotten on my travels, and I don't want to toss them. So I gift them to my friends, who seem quite happy with their new treasures.

One last bit of wisdom from The FlyLady: Focus on progress, not perfection. You will feel the benefits immediately. Decluttering is so liberating.

CHAPTER 27:

Relationship Challenges

Retirement can bring out the best or worst in a relationship. Let's start with reports from people on Reddit, who show the range of what can happen when you suddenly have all the time in the world with your significant other.

- "Our marriage 100% improved after retirement. We have separate interests, we have shared interests. The stress of children—especially when they were teens—was taxing. My husband was always very controlling with money, and I let it slide for years. In retirement, I told him he could still control the money but could never question one penny I spent or else I'd take my half and move on. After pouting for a couple of days, he chose the first option. Our 40-year battle of money was resolved. He has kept his promise. We are truly enjoying each other's company, and our golden years are indeed golden."

- "I'm no longer the grumpy bastard I was during the last few years that I worked a job I didn't enjoy. It's key that we balance activities that we enjoy together, with ample 'separate time' for our own hobbies and activities. We've definitely gotten closer."

- "Marriage has gotten worse during retirement. Being around a someone too much means you can get on each other's nerves. She took sex off the table nine years ago and so the bond is slowly dissolving."

- "We have really rekindled our romance. We always had a good marriage, but I picked up a couple of books by John Gottman (*The Seven Principles for Making Marriage Work*), a researcher in marital stability and happiness. We did some of the exercises together and we are much more conscious about being grateful for each other and in tune to each other's feelings. Plus, with no work stress and lots of time to relax, our sex life is wonderful."

- "We had too much time together, something that was totally fine for me because I thought she was my best friend. Unfortunately, it was too much for her. Of course, there were other factors that led to the divorce, but too much time together was the main cause."

- "When our kids finally moved out, we looked at each other and were happy to say we still liked each other. It keeps getting better and better. We are enjoying more travel, playing pickleball together, and more. We have also started developing more social engagements separate from each other. We rely on and enjoy each other, but we also have our own interests."

- "If there is any possibility of saving your marriage and living reasonably happy, I would say to do that first. Go for the couples counseling and make the big effort. I waited until retirement to divorce after 37 years. My wife got half of everything, which was fine. After years of me warning her that I wasn't happy, she wouldn't go to counseling and that was it. I'm enjoying the dating scene. I hadn't realized how much I missed someone being nice to me. If there is any hope of keeping your existing relationship, make the effort. If not, have hope for a better future and make the change. There may be a lot of very dark and depressing days filled with self-doubt, but you will get past them."

- "I got on my wife's nerves instantly because I was messing with her routine. We're starting to work it out. We have separate projects and interests. We do errands separately. I work out, she visits friends and family. Late afternoon, we are back together and acting normal. Weekends, we break routine and spend both days together. Otherwise, all the days would blend into each other."

- "It's just the two of us again and life is good! My husband and I are best friends. We like gardening, exercise, and travel, but we also have separate interests. We have to be so careful with our health and finances. There isn't much room for error, but we are so content with each other!"

- "It bothered me when she retired and was there all the time. I learned to live with it and now it's no big deal. The trick is not letting little stuff get under your skin."

- Retirement can bring significant changes to a relationship, and while it can be a fulfilling time, it also presents challenges that couples need to navigate. This may be a time when you have to redefine or renegotiate your roles within your relationship. That can hit everything from financial decisions to chore lists. That's just for starters.

- Retirement shakes everything up. Your old responsibilities are gone. So are those stresses. But they are replaced with new responsibilities and stresses that can test a relationship. If you retire at the same time, you both have to adjust to going from structured work schedules to wide-open calendars. Now you have to figure out what you want to do together and what you want to do independently. Both of you may have very different expectations on that. If one of you retires before the other, there may be feelings of disconnect, resentment, or imbalance in your relationship.

- At the same time, there are new financial issues. In some instances, it's a little stressful. In other situations, it is *very* stressful. Adjusting to a fixed income or changes in financial dynamics can stress a relationship, especially if you haven't adequately saved for retirement.

- All of this can hit one or both of you on a soul level. So many of us got purpose and identity from our work. When you lose that, you may struggle to redefine yourself. Not only are you trying to figure out what to do with your time, but you're also struggling with deep thoughts like, "Why am I here?" and "Who am I now?"

- At least you have each other, and hopefully, your connection will nurture you as you come to grips with changes in the amount of social interaction you get on an average day. Are you going to find new friends as couples or are you going to also get new connections to satisfy you solo?

- Quality time may be something you have dreamed of and wanted for years. But maybe not. Maybe you want a little space. How are you going to get it? Spending tons of time together can strengthen bonds, but it can also test them. It can feel suffocating if you don't have enough personal space or time to pursue what interests you.

- Addressing these challenges involves open communication, mutual respect, and a willingness to adapt to new circumstances. You and your significant other may have different expectations about how you want to spend your retirement years. Whether it's traveling, volunteering, or pursuing hobbies, aligning these expectations and finding common ground is crucial.

Tips for Protecting Your Relationship in Retirement

Communicate Openly and Honestly:
- Share your expectations and concerns about retirement.
- Regularly check in with each other to discuss how things are going and if any adjustments need to be made.

Maintain Individual Interests:

- Pursue hobbies and activities independently to ensure you both have personal space and fulfillment.
- Encourage each other to try new things or rekindle old passions.

Create a Routine:

- Establish a daily or weekly routine that includes time for shared activities and individual pursuits.
- Design a structure to provide a sense of purpose and normalcy.

Plan Together:

- Set goals and plan activities or trips that you can enjoy together.
- Collaborate on projects, whether it's home improvements, gardening, or volunteering.

Respect Each Other's Space:

- Recognize the importance of having time apart to recharge and maintain individuality.
- Accept that your partner's need for personal space is perfectly normal.
- Find separate areas in your home where you can retreat to relax or focus on personal interests.

Stay Active and Healthy:

- Incorporate physical activities into your routine, whether it's walking, swimming, or yoga.
- Cook and enjoy healthy meals together to maintain your well-being.

Socialize:

- Maintain and build social connections outside of your relationship.

- Join clubs, take classes, or participate in community events to meet new people and stay engaged.

Revisit Financial Plans:
- Regularly review your finances to ensure you're on track with your retirement goals.
- Seek advice from a financial adviser, if needed, to stay informed about your financial health.

Embrace Flexibility:
- Be open to adjusting your plans and routines as needed.
- This time in life involves ongoing tweaks to ensure both partners are happy.

Celebrate Milestones:
- Acknowledge and celebrate achievements and special moments, no matter how small.
- Create new traditions and cherish the time you have together.

Seek Support if Needed:
- Don't hesitate to seek counseling or support if you're facing challenges in your relationship.
- Therapy can provide valuable insights and help strengthen your bond.

Is Your Relationship Working?

This is a now-or-never moment in your life, especially if you have spent years settling for or hating your relationship. Please, please do not be impulsive about this. But this may be a last call for making a change if you have been unhappy for many years.

I'm including this quiz as a starting point to see if you need to spend time assessing what you want to do about your relationship situation. If you think you need to make a change, for goodness' sake, don't do it today! Get some therapy. Talk to your friends. Take some time.

But you are not stuck. You do have options. They may not be easy, but if you've been afraid to make the change you have known forever would make you happier, it's time to examine why you haven't done anything and if you need to shake things up.

Relationship Reflection Quiz for Retirees

Instructions: For each statement, rate how much you agree or disagree on a scale of 1 to 5.

1: Strongly Disagree

2: Disagree

3: Neutral

4: Agree

5: Strongly Agree

Part 1: Personal Happiness and Fulfillment

1. I feel genuinely happy and fulfilled in my current relationship.
2. My partner and I share similar life goals and values.
3. I feel respected and valued by my partner.
4. My relationship contributes positively to my overall well-being.
5. I feel emotionally supported by my partner in difficult times.

Part 2: Communication and Connection

6. My partner and I communicate openly and honestly with each other.
7. We can discuss difficult topics without arguments escalating.

8. I feel a deep emotional connection with my partner.

9. My partner and I enjoy spending quality time together.

10. We have similar interests and enjoy doing activities together.

Part 3: Independence and Growth

11. I feel free to pursue my own interests and hobbies outside of the relationship.

12. My partner encourages my personal growth and self-improvement.

13. I have my own social support network outside of my partner.

14. I feel that my partner and I grow together as individuals.

15. I feel a sense of autonomy and independence within my relationship.

Part 4: Concerns and Doubts

16. I often feel lonely or emotionally distant from my partner.

17. There are unresolved issues in our relationship that cause me distress.

18. I find myself fantasizing about life without my partner.

19. I am frequently frustrated or dissatisfied with my relationship.

20. I feel that my needs are not being met in this relationship.

Part 5: Long-Term Considerations

21. I can envision a happy future with my partner in the coming years.

22. I believe my relationship will improve with time and effort.

23. I feel I have to stay in this relationship, even if I'm not happy.

24. My partner and I have discussed our future together and are on the same page.

25. I worry about the impact of ending the relationship on my partner or family.

Scoring:

- **Mostly 1s and 2s:** Your relationship may be facing significant challenges, and it could be worth exploring whether continuing it is in your best interest. Consider speaking with a therapist or counselor.
- **Mostly 3s:** You may have mixed feelings about your relationship. Reflect on what changes could improve it or whether it's worth staying.
- **Mostly 4s and 5s:** Your relationship seems strong, and you likely find it fulfilling. If you have concerns, address them openly with your partner to strengthen your bond.

Next Steps:
- **Self-Reflection:** Take time to think about your answers and what they reveal about your relationship.
- **Communication:** Consider discussing the results with your partner. Open dialogue can often clarify feelings and lead to mutual understanding.
- **Professional Guidance:** If you're uncertain, talking to a relationship counselor or therapist can provide valuable insight.

Remember, this quiz is a tool for self-reflection and is not a substitute for professional advice. Ending a long-term relationship is a significant decision that should be made carefully and thoughtfully.

CHAPTER 28

Dating Again

I have to laugh at the idea of me giving advice on dating. It's been a rough road! Still, here many of us are, vibrant and unattached.

I have had people fix me up, and I've done online dating. Every time I stick my toe in the water, I take it out after a few weeks and wait a few years to try again.

Dating can be your ticket to companionship, love, or new friendships. It can also be fodder for stories that will have your friends crying with laughter. Oh yeah, I do have some stories!

You have to approach dating with an open heart and a sense of adventure. Whether it's a casual coffee date or a romantic dinner, each experience is a chance to learn and grow. If you're lucky, you find somebody wonderful immediately and don't have to do it for long, but that's generally not how it works. I just tell myself I am out there doing research for a novel.

Know what you want. I want somebody who is no more than four years older than me (I don't want to be a nurse or a purse, as the saying goes), who is honest, politically moderate, loves God, is rabid about the outdoors and the water, active, physically fit, healthy, financially set . . . See? It's a tall order!

Think about what you're looking for. Are you seeking companionship, romance, or just someone to do things with? It's important to be honest with yourself and potential partners about your intentions. This clarity will help you attract people who are looking for the same thing.

Dating should be fun and fulfilling, but it's also important to take care of your emotional well-being. . If you've been through a tough breakup, loss, or significant change, make sure you are emotionally ready to start dating again. It's okay to take your time. Self-care isn't just a buzzword; it's the foundation for healthy relationships.

Online dating might seem daunting at first, especially if it's new to you. But it's a fantastic way to meet people who share your interests and values. Start by choosing a dating site or app that caters to seniors, but beware. Sometimes, the most wonderful people will respond, but they aren't real. They're after your money. More on that in a bit.

Here's how to get started:
- Create a Profile: Take some time to write a profile that reflects who you are. Be honest, positive, and specific about your interests and what you're looking for in a partner. A friendly, smiling profile picture goes a long way too! Post pictures of yourself doing the activities you want the other person to do with you.
- Be Safe: Online dating is generally safe, but it's important to stay cautious. Don't share personal information like your address too soon. Do NOT share your financial information. Always meet in a public place for the first few dates, and let someone close to you know where you'll be.
- Take Your Time: Don't feel pressured to respond to every message or rush into anything. Take your time to get to know the person through messages and phone calls before meeting in person. Some people will immediately ask you to get together for coffee or a drink. Don't do it!

When you do get together, be yourself. At this stage in your life, you have a clear sense of who you are, so don't feel the need to pretend otherwise. Authenticity is key to forming meaningful connections.

Your ideal partner might not come in the package you expect. They might have different interests or come from a different background. Be open to getting to know people who don't fit your usual "type." You might be pleasantly surprised by who you connect with. (I always get tripped up on this)

Remember, dating is supposed to be fun! It's an opportunity to meet new people, explore new activities, and rediscover yourself. Don't put too much pressure on any one date. If it works out, great! If not, it's material for your novel! Not every date will lead to a long-term relationship, and that's okay. Don't get discouraged. The right person is out there, and each step brings you closer to finding love.

I wish I didn't have to emphasize this, but I've seen many people get sucked in and ripped off by online fakes who take their money, then disappear. If something feels off about the person you're chatting with, pay attention to that feeling. Red flags are too-good-to-be-true situations or vague responses to your questions. Beware if someone is reluctant to meet in person or video chat. A real person who is interested in you will want to connect face-to-face at some point. If they keep making excuses, it's a warning sign. "Catfishers"—or impostors—often avoid video calls because they don't look like the photos they're using.

Check their photos. Use reverse image search tools like Google Images to see if their pictures are taken from someone else's profile or stock images. If their photos appear on multiple sites under different names, that's a huge red flag.

My friend wanted me to check out a man her friend was sending money to. She sent me his Facebook profile and I did a reverse image search on Google Images. There were *fifteen* Facebook profiles with the same image. Catfish!

Be wary of sob stories or sudden emergencies that lead to requests for money. A common tactic of catfishers is to pretend to build an emotional connection, then ask for financial help. No matter how convincing the story is, avoid sending money to someone you haven't met in person.

Another friend knows a woman who, months after her husband's sudden death, connected with a man who conned her into selling her house, putting the money in her bank account, and giving him the account information. I have no idea how this turned out because, when her friends raised red flags, she stopped talking to them.

Look at the person's social media presence. A lack of a digital footprint or having only a few friends or followers is suspicious. Most real people have some sort of online history.

Finally, talk to someone you trust about your online relationship. Sometimes, an outsider's perspective can help you see things you might be missing.

Staying cautious and doing a bit of detective work can save you from the heartache of being ripped off and broken-hearted. If you spot the warning signs, it's okay to walk away. Better safe than sorry!

Dating again as a senior can be a joyful and enriching experience. There are highs, and there are lows. Embrace this opportunity with an open heart and mind, and remember that it's never too late to find love or companionship. Be patient with yourself, enjoy the journey, and trust that good things are on the horizon.

CHAPTER 29

The Power of Ritual and Routine

Feeling unmoored now that you have all the time in the world? You can create stability by designing a routine to give you direction throughout your day. After years of structured days filled with work, deadlines, and responsibilities, the sudden openness of retirement can be both exhilarating and daunting. This is where the power of ritual and routine comes in.

Creating a daily routine in retirement isn't about restricting your newfound freedom; it's about finding balance and purpose in this new chapter of your life.

For some people, rituals and routines offer a sense of stability and comfort. They give shape to the day and provide a rhythm that can help you feel more grounded and focused. Whether it's starting your morning with a quiet cup of coffee, going for a walk, or spending time on a favorite hobby, these small, intentional actions can make a big difference in how you experience each day.

One of the beautiful things about retirement is that you get to decide what your routine looks like. This is your time to craft a life that reflects your passions, interests, and values. The key is to find a balance between structure and spontaneity—enough routine to give your days a sense of flow but with the flexibility to enjoy new experiences and opportunities as they arise.

Start by thinking about what matters most to you. What activities bring you joy or a sense of accomplishment? Maybe you love gardening, reading, volunteering, or spending time with family and friends. These are the things that can form the foundation of your daily routine.

Consider your mornings first, because the way you start your day often sets the tone for the rest of it. You might begin with some quiet time—meditation, journaling, or simply enjoying the sunrise. This can be followed by some physical activity, like a walk or a gentle workout, to get your body moving and your energy up. Having a consistent morning routine can help you feel more focused and positive as you move through the day.

As your day unfolds, try to mix in different types of activities. Try to find things that stimulate your mind, keep you physically active, and nurture your social connections. For example, you might spend an hour or two on a hobby, take a class, or meet a friend for lunch. Variety in your routine keeps things interesting and fulfilling.

Evenings can be a time to wind down, perhaps with a good book, a favorite TV show, or a relaxing bath. Creating a bedtime ritual can also help you get better sleep, which is so important for overall well-being.

Remember, your routine doesn't have to be rigid. It should evolve as you do, changing with the seasons or as new interests develop. The goal is to create a rhythm that supports your physical, mental, and emotional health, allowing you to enjoy this time in your life to the fullest.

"Those who think they have no time for bodily exercise will sooner
or later have to find time for illness."
—British Statesman Edward Stanley

"At age 20, we worry about what others think of us.
At age 40, we don't care what they think of us.
At age 60, we discover they haven't been thinking of us at all."
—Legendary Advice Columnist Ann Landers

CHAPTER 30:

Alcoholism and Addiction

As the structure and routine of daily work life disappear, some retirees find themselves struggling to fill the void. Sometimes, this leads to unhealthy and self-destructive habits.

Alcohol, in particular, can become a significant issue. Studies show that alcohol use often increases in retirement, with some people drinking more frequently or in larger quantities than they did when they were still working. According to the National Institute on Alcohol Abuse and Alcoholism, about 14 percent of older adults binge drink, and this number is on the rise. The sense of loss that can come without your old sense of purpose, social connections, and daily routine can lead you to use alcohol as a way to cope with loneliness, boredom, or even depression.

The problem is that as we age, our bodies become more sensitive to alcohol, and the risks associated with drinking increase. What might have felt like a harmless habit in earlier years can quickly spiral into something more dangerous. Alcohol can exacerbate health issues common in older adults, such as high blood pressure, diabetes, and memory problems. It can also interact with medications, leading to serious side effects.

But it's not just alcohol. Other addictions, like prescription medications, gambling, or even overeating can also become more problematic during retirement. The sudden change in lifestyle can create a vacuum, and without the structure of work, some people turn to these behaviors as a way to fill the time or escape their feelings of unease.

If that is happening to you, be aware of the signs of addiction. Talk openly about the struggles of retirement, including the emotional and psychological impacts. That can help reduce the stigma and make it easier for you to seek help.

There are also many resources available, from counseling and support groups to programs specifically designed for older adults dealing with addiction. Reaching out for help is not a sign of weakness, but a brave and necessary step toward a healthier, more fulfilling retirement.

And again, this is not uncommon. The big question is if you are going to do something about it.

Quiz: Identifying Signs of Addiction

1. **Routine and Daily Habits:**
    *   Have you found yourself drinking alcohol or using substances more frequently since you retired?
        *   a) Yes
        *   b) No
    *   Do you often start your day or end your evening with a drink or substance use?
        *   a) Yes
        *   b) No
    *   Has your daily routine shifted significantly, with more time spent alone or in isolation?
        *   a) Yes
        *   b) No

2. **Physical and Health Changes:**
   - Have you noticed a need to increase your intake to achieve the same level of relaxation or enjoyment?
     - a) Yes
     - b) No
   - Are you experiencing new or worsening health issues, such as high blood pressure, memory problems, or sleep disturbances?
     - a) Yes
     - b) No
   - Do you often feel unwell, anxious, or jittery when not using alcohol or a particular substance?
     - a) Yes
     - b) No

3. **Emotional Well-being:**
   - Have you noticed changes in your mood, such as irritability, anxiety, or depression?
     - a) Yes
     - b) No
   - Do you use alcohol or other substances to cope with feelings of loneliness, boredom, or sadness?
     - a) Yes
     - b) No
   - Have you lost interest in hobbies or activities you once enjoyed?
     - a) Yes
     - b) No

4. **Social and Financial Indicators:**
   - Have your relationships with family or friends become strained, perhaps due to concerns about your drinking or substance use?
     - a) Yes
     - b) No
   - Are you spending more money than usual on alcohol, gambling, or other potentially addictive behaviors?
     - a) Yes
     - b) No
   - Have you found yourself avoiding social situations unless alcohol or a particular substance is involved?
     - a) Yes
     - b) No

Results:
- **Mostly Yes:** If you answered "Yes" to several of these questions, it may be an indication of a developing addiction. It's important to seek support, whether from loved ones, a healthcare provider, or a support group.
- **Mostly No:** If you answered "No" to most questions, you may not be experiencing signs of addiction, but continue to monitor your habits and emotions, especially during the transition into retirement.

*"You know you're an alcoholic when
you misplace things—like a decade."*
— Paul Williams

*"The chains of habit are too light to be
felt until they are too heavy to be broken."*
— Warren Buffett

*"First you take a drink, then the drink takes a drink,
then the drink takes you."*
— F. Scott Fitzgerald

CHAPTER 31:

Senior Moments

I was in deep conversation with my best friend, Joyce, but my mind stopped, cold. I struggled in my head. *What was I talking about? What? WHAT?*

Finally, I had to say what I've said too many times to too many people. "I'm sorry. What was I talking about?" I asked.

"It doesn't matter," she said kindly. "We'll forget it anyway."

Here we are in the forgetfulness zone. We blame our lapses on senior moments, but the more frequently they occur, the more we wonder if something more serious, like Alzheimer's disease or dementia, is taking over our brains.

I had to face this head-on three years ago after a serious concussion after a cycling accident wiped out part of my memory. I was unable to work for a few months, and the lapses continued for more than a year. The low point came when a neurologist told me it was likely early onset Alzheimer's or dementia. I was devastated. It took months of testing to get to the truth: It wasn't either of those nightmare diagnoses that I so feared would condemn me to a long goodbye like my mother had suffered. What I had was a really bad concussion. That experience made me realize what was at stake and how difficult decisions were going to be if I had to plan a future being single with Alzheimer's or dementia.

Fortunately, my memory has recovered now, except when I get senior moments. They happen all the time. I forget what I'm talking about, I forget names, I forget what I went to get in another room. I work on my memory, sometimes by doing math problems, sometimes with trivia. I've trained myself to never resort to Google for an answer to something my brain can't immediately retrieve. I have to make my brain work.

I take ginkgo biloba every morning and magnesium L-threonate because the latest research says they help with memory.

When you think your number has suddenly come up and you are going to drift into that diagnosis, you wish you'd devoted yourself to doing sudoku and learning new languages instead of watching YouTube and scrolling Instagram. If you don't have that diagnosis, do yourself a favor and do what you can to insulate yourself from that kind of decline. I watched my mother suffer that fate for twelve years, and I need to do everything I can to make sure that does not happen to me. You should too. Do it with me, because if there is something you can do to ward it off, YOU SHOULD DO IT.

First, let's talk about the basics: diet and exercise. Eating a balanced diet rich in fruits, vegetables, whole grains, and lean proteins can fuel your brain. Foods rich in antioxidants, like berries and nuts, are particularly beneficial. Research shows that plant-based or vegan diets are best. Regular exercise is equally important. Physical activity increases blood flow to your brain, which can help keep your memory in shape. Even a daily walk can make a difference.

Mental exercise is just as crucial. Challenge your brain with puzzles, games, or learning new skills. Try crosswords, sudoku, or even learning a new language. These activities can help form new neural connections, keeping your brain agile and engaged. Reading books, engaging in stimulating conversations, and even taking up new hobbies can also give your brain a much-needed workout.

Staying organized is another key strategy. Keep a calendar or planner to jot down important dates and tasks. Use sticky notes around the house for reminders. Setting up a routine can help, too. Doing things at the same time each day makes it easier to remember them. And don't forget your phone—it's a great tool for setting alarms and reminders for everything from taking medication to calling a friend.

Staying socially active is incredibly beneficial. Regular social interaction can boost your mood and memory. Join clubs, volunteer, or simply make it a point to catch up with friends and family. Engaging with others keeps your brain focused and can help stave off feelings of isolation, which can negatively impact memory.

Sleep is crucial. Make sure you're getting enough restful sleep each night. Sleep is when your brain consolidates memories and processes information from the day. Aim for seven to nine hours per night and try to maintain a regular sleep schedule. I used to get five or six hours a night and thought that was plenty. When I upped it to seven, my memory instantly sharpened. I hope to one day work up to eight hours.

Finally, stress management is critical. Chronic stress can take a toll on your memory. Techniques like meditation, deep breathing exercises, and yoga can help you manage stress effectively. Even simple activities like walking in nature, listening to music, or practicing mindfulness can make a big difference.

If your forgetfulness is interfering with your daily life, it might be time to talk to your doctor to see what's going on. Hopefully, you are just experiencing senior moments.

Embrace these changes as part of a healthy, balanced lifestyle, and you'll likely find that you're remembering things with ease and enjoying life to the fullest.

If you lose where you are in a conversation every now and again, if you forget why you walked into a room or why you called someone, you're probably just dealing with senior moments. And, like Joyce said, "It doesn't matter. We're going to forget it anyhow."

Quiz: Are You Losing It?

Let's start with a big fat caveat. This quiz is no substitute for a neurological exam or professional psychological assessment. This will not determine if you have Alzheimer's disease or dementia. But it may let you know if you have a problem—or not. For each question, choose the option that best describes the frequency or severity of the symptom.

Memory Loss:

a) Rarely forget things.

b) Occasionally forget things but usually remember later.

c) Frequently forget recent events and important dates.

Difficulty Performing Familiar Tasks:

a) No difficulty performing daily tasks.

b) Sometimes have trouble with complex tasks (e.g., managing finances).

c) Often have trouble with familiar tasks like cooking or driving to familiar locations.

Language Problems:

a) Rarely have trouble finding the right word.

b) Occasionally struggle to find the right word but eventually do.

c) Frequently have difficulty finding words or following conversations.

Disorientation to Time and Place:

a) Always know the date and location.

b) Occasionally forget the day of the week or get lost in unfamiliar places.

c) Often forget the date or time or become lost in familiar places.

Poor Judgment:

a) Make decisions with good judgment.

b) Occasionally make poor decisions.

c) Frequently make poor decisions or inappropriate choices.

Misplacing Things:

a) Rarely misplace items.

b) Sometimes misplace items but can usually retrace steps to find them.

c) Frequently misplace items and cannot find them, sometimes putting them in unusual places.

Changes in Mood and Behavior:

a) Mood and behavior are consistent.

b) Occasionally experience mood swings or changes in behavior.

c) Frequently experience mood swings, anxiety, or depression.

Loss of Initiative:

a) Remain active and involved in activities.

b) Occasionally feel less interested in activities.

c) Often withdraw from work or social activities.

Problems with Abstract Thinking:

a) Have no difficulty with abstract thinking (e.g., balancing a checkbook).

b) Occasionally have trouble with complex thoughts.

c) Frequently have difficulty with abstract thinking and problem-solving.

Trouble Understanding Visual and Spatial Relationships:

a) Have no trouble judging distance or understanding visual information.

b) Occasionally have difficulty with depth perception or visual details.

c) Frequently have trouble with visual and spatial relationships, such as judging distances or recognizing faces.

Scoring:

Mostly A's: These are typical signs of normal aging. Occasional lapses in memory and changes in behavior are common.

Mostly B's: These symptoms could indicate mild cognitive impairment, which may be an early sign of dementia or Alzheimer's. Monitoring symptoms and consulting a healthcare professional for evaluation is advisable.

Mostly C's: These are more concerning symptoms that may indicate dementia or Alzheimer's disease. It is important to seek a professional medical evaluation for a thorough assessment.

Remember, this quiz is not a diagnostic tool. If you or someone you know is experiencing these symptoms, it's important to seek advice from a healthcare provider for an accurate diagnosis and appropriate intervention.

Need to Jog Your Memory?
Here are some effective techniques to help jog your memory:

Immediate Techniques

1. **Retrace Your Steps**: Go back to the place where you last remember having the thought or object.
2. **Relax**: Stress can block memory recall. Take deep breaths or a short break.
3. **Use Contextual Cues**: Think about related details, such as what you were doing or who you were with.

Mnemonic Devices

1. **Acronyms**: Create an acronym from the first letters of the words you want to remember.

2. **Visualization**: Create a vivid mental image associated with the information.

3. **Rhymes and Songs**: Turn the information into a rhyme or a song.

Association Techniques

1. **Linking**: Connect new information to something you already know.

2. **Storytelling**: Create a story that includes the information you want to remember.

Organizational Tools

1. **Write it Down**: Jot down notes or make lists to help you remember.

2. **Use Technology**: Set reminders or use apps designed for memory support.

Mental Exercises

3. **Memory Games**: Engage in activities like puzzles, card games, or memory apps.

4. **Regular Practice**: Regularly challenge your brain with new information and activities.

Healthy Habits

5. **Stay Active**: Physical exercise can improve brain function and memory.

6. **Balanced Diet**: Eat a diet rich in omega-3 fatty acids, antioxidants, and other brain-healthy nutrients.

7. **Get Adequate Sleep**: Ensure you get enough sleep, as it is crucial for memory consolidation.

Social Interaction

8. **Talk It Out**: Discuss what you're trying to remember with someone else.

9. **Stay Connected**: Regular social interaction can keep your mind engaged and improve memory.

Regular Practice

10. **Repetition**: Repeating information several times can help reinforce it in your memory.

11. **Teach Others**: Teaching someone else what you're trying to remember can help solidify the information.

By combining these techniques, you can effectively jog your memory and improve your recall abilities.

CHAPTER 32:

Go-go, Slow-go, and No-go

The first time I heard the line about the phases of retirement being divided into "Go-go, Slow-go, and No-go," I thought it was a great joke.

Well, the joke is on us. Those three distinct phases of retirement are real, and they impact our lifestyle, activity level, and overall well-being.

The "Go-go" days are the "salad days" of retirement—the early years of our liberation from work when, hopefully, we've still got our health, verve, and energy. Generally, this phase starts right as we leave the workforce when we are enthusiastic and eager to try new experiences, travel, and do what we have postponed during our working years. Many of us fill this time with fitness and hobbies, starting new businesses, or volunteering. The moniker "Go-go" reflects the active and vibrant lifestyle of the freedom in our new lives.

But that doesn't last forever. The "Slow-go" phase is a transition where we do less physical activity and slide into a more relaxed pace of life. While still active and engaged, retirees in the Slow-go phase may start to scale back on more physically demanding activities or rigorous travel. This is because of our health. The shift may mean focusing on maintaining well-being and possibly managing chronic health conditions. But in Slow-go, we are still going. Despite the slower pace, many of us continue to enjoy social interactions, hobbies, and community activities. But there's been a shift.

And finally, the "No-go" phase, which, let's face it, a lot of us would prefer to skip. This is the last stage, when physical limitations and health issues may significantly restrict our mobility and daily activities. During this phase, we may find ourselves spending more time at home and relying more on others for assistance with daily tasks. Social circles may shrink, especially as our friends start to pass away or if mobility issues prevent regular participation in social activities. While some of us may experience feelings of isolation or frustration due to reduced independence, others find ways to adapt by focusing on more sedentary hobbies, connecting virtually with family and friends, or seeking support from community services and healthcare professionals.

These phases of retirement are not strictly linear or universally experienced in the same way by everyone. Change can happen gradually or in an instant. Factors such as health, financial stability, personal interests, and support systems can influence how we navigate each phase. Additionally, advancements in healthcare and lifestyle choices can extend active and independent living well into the later years.

I'd prefer to go from "Go-go" to the great beyond, but I don't know if I will get that luxury. I try to be proactive with my health and well-being so I can enjoy a quality of life for as long as possible. But age catches up with everyone who doesn't die young, so it's on us to make the decision whether we are going to cope with these transitions—or not.

There's going to be a lot of transitioning, and that can be physically and psychologically challenging. The better we adapt, the better these transitions will be. But it's never going to be easy. I will never forget Cher and the legendary Tina

Turner on Oprah years ago. Oprah looked at the divas and commented on Cher being 61 and Tina being 68 at the time.

"How do you feel about getting older?"

"I think it sucks!" Cher blurted.

Tina burst out laughing.

"What about all the wisdom . . ." Oprah said.

"Oh f**k that!" Cher said, bursting out laughing.

Who wants to roll into the "No-go" stage? But, as plenty of older people say, "It beats the alternative."

Throughout these transitions, maintaining a positive mindset is critical. Staying connected to social networks can support your emotional well-being, but don't fall into the trap of endless discussion of medical problems and how much it sucks to get older. Engaging in meaningful activities, whether physical or intellectual, can help you feel purpose and fulfillment. Additionally, staying proactive about health through regular medical check-ups, physical activity appropriate for your abilities, as well as a balanced diet can contribute to overall well-being and longevity.

Family and community support are vital through these transitions. Open communication and understanding among family members can facilitate discussions about future care needs and preferences. Community resources like senior centers, support groups, or home care services can provide valuable assistance and companionship.

Ultimately, adapting to each phase of retirement with grace will allow you to make the most of your later years. When you slow down, you can still read, write, listen to audios, watch movies, talk to people, and do a lot. But you can't do what you used to do. My pharmacist father, whom I mentioned earlier in this book, was still studying the latest drugs until a few days before he died. It gave him purpose.

All of this is why it is so important to get while the getting is good. If you've got your health, celebrate it! If you're strong enough to do adventures, do adventures!

If you are able enough to travel, get out there and travel! You know you can do it right now, so it's on you to do it right now. You don't get a memo telling you the date you are going to switch to the next phase. Life just happens.

Stuck at Home in Slow-go and No-go

You may be enjoying the Go-go phase when something suddenly happens to ground you. You break your ankle, get some other body part replaced, or even have heart surgery that you will ultimately rebound from. But you'll be merrily living your life and suddenly be grounded in place, at home, with none of your normal activity or stimulation. As we go through life into the Slow-Go and No-Go phases, we have to make peace with more or even all of our time being limited to staying in place at home. We get grounded as we recuperate from surgeries or illnesses, and it becomes more common the older we get and our bodies undergo natural wear and tear. Eventually, we may be stuck in place until the end.

As our physical capability declines, routine activities can become challenging. This physical frailty can result in increased susceptibility to falls or injuries, further necessitating periods of rest and recuperation at home.

Who wants that? Nobody. But we have to face it. Being homebound can lead to feelings of loneliness, isolation, and even depression, especially if the confinement is prolonged or recurring.

Being stuck at home does not equate to idleness or a lack of productivity. Smart older adults use this time to engage in hobbies, pursue lifelong interests, or even explore new ones to keep themselves engaged. That engagement keeps them going. Homebound periods can provide an opportunity for reflection, self-care, and reconnection with loved ones through technology or visits from family and friends.

None of us can pretend that doing a jigsaw puzzle at home is remotely as fun as a nice trip to Paris, but you have got to find activities to keep you engaged so you don't lose your mind.

CHAPTER 33:

Stay-Busy Activities When You are Homebound

When you're homebound, the world may feel like it has shrunk to the size of your living room, but you can find a way to create adventure within those walls. There are so many ways to fill your days with joy, creativity, and connection without ever stepping outside. Consider:

- Watercolor or oil painting
- Read short stories
- Bake
- Listen to music
- Watch classic movies
- Gardening (indoor plants)
- Do simple crosswords
- Play with clay or playdough
- Birdwatch from a window

- Color in adult coloring books
- Knit or crochet
- Watch documentaries
- Look through photo albums
- Do simple yoga
- Listen to audiobooks
- Play card games
- Do word searches
- Arrange flowers
- Scented candle therapy
- Sewing projects
- Make homemade ice cream
- Paint rocks
- Scrapbooking
- Watch comedy shows
- Build things with LEGO
- Woodworking
- Do chair exercises
- Put together a memory box
- Make jewelry
- Draw with art pencils
- Play with your pet
- Organize family recipes
- Watch sports highlights
- Play simple board games
- Write letters to friends
- Create a vision board
- Do armchair travel on YouTube
- Play musical instruments

- Watch cooking shows
- Make a family tree
- Do hand massages
- Explore Google Earth
- Make homemade candles
- Craft with beads
- Listen to guided meditations
- Organize your bookshelf
- Sing karaoke
- Write a daily journal
- Do math problems
- Dance
- Watch animal cams online
- Plant seeds
- Do chair tai chi
- Watch family videos
- Do simple origami
- Learn sign language
- Write poetry
- Create handmade cards
- Make bird feeders
- Learn simple magic tricks
- Listen to classical music
- Play online trivia games
- Make a gratitude list
- Make a family cookbook
- Create a time capsule
- Stretch
- Explore family history

- Paint by numbers
- Listen to storytelling podcasts
- Do simple DIY projects
- Do memory games

Affirmations for When You Are Stuck at Home

- My home is a safe and comforting place.
- I am grateful I have time to rest and restore my health.
- I am patient with myself.
- I embrace this time to focus on self-care, remember good times, and embrace my spirituality.
- I am surrounded by love and support from my family and friends.
- I am resilient, and I adapt to challenges with grace and courage.
- I choose positivity and find joy in each day.

"It is not how old you are, but how you are old."
— Jules Renard

"Wisdom comes with winters."
— Oscar Wilde

"With age, comes wisdom. With wisdom, comes a slowing down of life and an
appreciation of what truly matters."
— Unknown

"The longer I live, the more I realize that as I age,
I value peace and serenity over excitement and thrill."
— Unknown

"Aging is an extraordinary process where you
become the person you always should have been."
— David Bowie

CHAPTER 34

Losing Loved Ones

One of the hardest parts of growing older is losing our friends and loved ones. Each loss leaves a mark on our hearts, an empty space that once was filled with laughter, memories, and connection.

It can feel like there's less light around us with each person who passes. The people we lose are more than just friends or family; they are the threads that weave our lives together. Losing them feels like losing pieces of ourselves.

As we age, the losses keep piling up. Funerals, memorials, and celebrations of life were once rare occurrences, but they become a regular part of life as we age. Each goodbye feels heavier because it's not just about losing one person—it's about all the losses that came before. Grief becomes a constant, always lurking in the background, ready to remind us of who we've lost.

Through this, we can also focus on gratitude. For everyone we lose, there are countless moments of joy, love, and connection that they brought into our lives. These memories become treasures to hold onto when the sadness feels overwhelming. We remember the way they laughed, the wisdom they shared, and the comfort of their presence.

It's important to allow ourselves to grieve and feel the pain and sadness that comes with loss. There's no timeline for grief and no right way to do it. Some days will be harder than others, and that's okay. What matters is that we honor our feelings and give ourselves the space to heal.

One of the most difficult parts of losing so many loved ones is the loneliness that can follow. It can feel like the world is getting smaller and there are fewer people who truly understand us. But even in this loneliness, there is the potential to find and create new connections. While no one can replace the friends and loved ones we've lost, we still have opportunities for new relationships and for finding comfort in others who are also navigating the complexities of aging and loss.

While aging may bring the pain of loss, it also brings a deeper appreciation for the love we've experienced and the people who have shaped our lives. We carry them with us, always.

Affirmations for Facing Loss

- I allow myself to grieve in my own time and way.
- I cherish the connections I had with my friends and carry their spirit with me.
- I am resilient and find strength and comfort during times of loss.
- I focus on the positive impact my friends had on my life rather than the pain of their absence.
- I am grateful for the friendships I have had and continue to form new, meaningful friendships.

"To age gracefully is to embrace all the moments of your life, to be fully present, and to understand the value of slowing down."
— Unknown

"Time may wrinkle the skin,
but to give up enthusiasm wrinkles the soul."
— Samuel Ullman

"Death is not the greatest loss in life. The greatest loss is what dies inside us while we live."
— Norman Cousins

"While I thought that I was learning how to live, I have been learning how to die."
— Leonardo da Vinci

CHAPTER 35:

Facing Your Own Mortality

Sooner or later, it hits you. Your time here is limited, and it is running out. With that realization comes a mix of emotions—fear, sadness, and sometimes even regret.

Grappling with mortality doesn't have to be a dark and lonely experience. It can also be a time of profound reflection and, ultimately, acceptance. One of the most powerful ways to cope with the reality of your mortality is to find meaning in your life as it is right now. The idea that your time is limited can inspire you to live more fully, to appreciate each day, and to focus on what truly matters. Instead of worrying about what you haven't done, you can start to cherish what you have—a loving family, close friends, memories of adventures, and even the small, everyday moments that bring you joy.

It's also important to acknowledge the fear and uncertainty that can come with thinking about your own mortality. It's natural to feel anxious about the unknown, about what comes after we are gone, or about how your life will be remembered. Talking about these fears with someone you trust—a friend, family member, or a therapist—can be incredibly helpful. Sometimes just saying the words out loud can ease the burden and make you feel less alone in your thoughts.

As you age, your priorities can shift, and that's a good thing. You might find yourself less concerned with material success or superficial goals and more focused on relationships, adventures, and your legacy.

Another way to cope with the reality of your mortality is to practice acceptance. This doesn't mean giving up or feeling defeated, but rather coming to peace with the fact that life is finite. This acceptance can lead to a deeper sense of calm and contentment. Instead of fighting against the inevitable, you can learn to embrace it as a natural part of life.

Finally, finding comfort in spirituality or a belief system can be a source of great solace. Whether it's a religious faith, a belief in an afterlife, or simply a connection to something greater than yourself, these beliefs can provide comfort and give you a sense of peace.

Ultimately, dealing with your mortality is about acknowledging the reality of your limited time while also celebrating the life you have left to live. It's about focusing on love, connection, and the simple joys of each day, knowing that in doing so, you are living your life fully with meaning and grace.

"The fear of death follows from the fear of life.
Someone who lives fully is prepared to die at any time."
— Mark Twain

"To the well-organized mind, death is but the next great adventure."
— J.K. Rowling

"Every man's life ends the same way. It is only the details of how he lived
and how he died that distinguish one man from another."
— Ernest Hemingway

When Your Health Starts to Go South

Facing health challenges as you age can be one of the most difficult aspects of growing older. Your body, which once seemed so strong and capable, will start to slow down, and you may find yourself dealing with aches, pains, and conditions that you never imagined. It can be frustrating, even frightening, to realize that you are not as invincible as you once thought.

It's easy to get angry or feel defeated when your body doesn't work the way you want it to. But those feelings, while valid, can make it harder to cope. Instead, you can try to be gentle with yourself, recognizing that aging is a natural part of life and it's okay to have limitations.

Staying connected with your healthcare providers and being proactive about your health is another key part of dealing with these challenges. Get regular check-ups. Take medications as prescribed. Report any symptoms you are experiencing. Work with your body and do what you can to stay as healthy as possible.

Support from loved ones is also crucial. Whether it's a spouse, children, friends, or even a support group, having people to talk to and lean on can provide comfort and strength. Sometimes just knowing that you are not alone in your struggle can lighten the burden. It's okay to ask for help, to admit that you are having a tough time, and to lean on those who care about you.

It's also important to find joy and purpose, even in the face of health challenges. This might mean adapting your activities to fit your new reality. Maybe you can't run marathons anymore, but you can enjoy a walk in the park, do some gardening, or spend time with loved ones. Finding new ways to experience pleasure and fulfillment can help you maintain a positive outlook, even when your health isn't what it used to be.

Finally, remember that your worth isn't tied to your physical ability. You are more than your body—you are the love you give, the wisdom you've gained, and the relationships you have nurtured over a lifetime. Dealing with health challenges is hard, but it doesn't have to diminish the richness in your life.

Affirmations for Dealing with Health Challenges

- I am resilient. My body heals and adapts.
- I am becoming stronger and healthier every day.
- I focus on what I can control and let go of what I can't.
- It is easy for me to ask for help from others.
- My health challenges do not define me; I am more than my illnesses.
- I nourish my body with healthy choices.
- I am surrounded by love and support.
- I trust in the journey of my life and am hopeful about my future.
- I embrace every day with positivity and gratitude.

CHAPTER 36:

Speaking about Health . . . DON'T.

Certain older people prattle on endlessly about how their bodies are falling apart. Years ago, I went to see some older neighbors and inquired how they were feeling. They started telling me. Every one of them went into a loop about whatever diagnosis or issue they were dealing with, and many of these situations were not crises. A younger neighbor leaned over and whispered into my ear, "You had to ask."

After that, I started noticing how quickly a lot of older people can get on a roll about every ache, pain, doctor visit, and real (or imagined) malaise.

As I started getting older, I noticed my friends had started doing it, too. Why, why, *why* were aches, pains, and constipation suddenly the go-to topics of conversation? We were still in our 50s when this started! But so many of my friends stopped talking about living and refocused on aches, pains, insurance, CPAP machines, blood pressure readings, and upcoming surgeries.

My theory is, the first few times things go wrong with our bodies, it's a shock. Everything always works, but then something doesn't. We're so bewildered that we have to talk about it.

Then something happens to a friend, and then another friend, and they are also shocked and have to talk about it. Then the more things happen, the more they share. Suddenly, the whole gang is in that same loop my neighbors were in. Especially for people who don't have much going on in their lives, medical issues are the only news du jour. It gives them something to report.

The problem is, the more we think and talk about it, the more our health issues take over our brains. Excessive ruminating and talking makes us think our medical issues are worse than they are. The more we talk about it, the more we think about it. The more we think about it, the more, more, more we think about it.

If something is really wrong, by all means, share it! You need your friends to guide you through true health crises. What I'm saying is that it's on you to manage your focus so a routine health matter does not become a crisis in your head.

If I have a health issue, I will discuss it when it needs to be discussed. Unless it's something significant and I need support, I will tell my closest friend and maybe my brother. But I don't need to tell fifty people when I have a cold or need an MRI. I just suck it up and then get on with living a wonderful life.

I think our friends should all write their medical issues down on index cards. When we go to dinner, we should pass the cards around, read them, and then acknowledge each person's card with a nod. If the issue is important and needs to be discussed, we absolutely should discuss it. But we need to be more deliberate about the conversation and take charge of complaining and negativity, because the older we get, the more we'll have to complain about.

Let's just make a conscious decision to not become a bunch of cranky old people who gripe about everything. Someone with cancer should be able to talk about the treatment and concerns as much as he or she wants. But someone with arthritis in a joint needs to go get acupuncture or physical therapy, do some aqua aerobics, and stay positive. We're getting older. We are responsible for our thoughts and attitudes.

Stay out of the loop on this.

CHAPTER 37:

Riding into the Sunset

I wish for you a great life—and a great death.

Reconnect with people. Strengthen bonds with loved ones. Try to create peace with people you believe have wronged you. Find closure now—because you still can. You have a choice about how you want to live. Deepen your relationships, not your resentments. Resolve conflicts and seek forgiveness where it is needed. Let go of grudges. Live in peace.

Get better at mindfulness, because that will amplify the experiences you have. Be present in each moment. Appreciate the beauty of life because all you can count on is what you have right now in this moment.

You have time now. Explore and deepen your spirituality. Create peace within yourself, either through prayer or meditation. That will reduce fear and anxiety through every stage of aging.

When you feel challenged, take a time-out for gratitude and focus on what you are thankful for. That is calming and affirming.

Share your wisdom, knowledge, and experiences with those who care about you or who could learn from you.

You're here now, so fill this moment with life. It's now or never, so travel, create your art, hike with vigor, and go outside for the sunset. Do what you have always wanted to do.

Fulfill yourself by filling your heart with life.

Don't leave this earth with a single regret.

ACKNOWLEDGMENTS

To Joyce Duarte, my bestie, who helps me make sense of the insanity of what is happening to us. To my close friend Tina Proctor who is 15 years older than me and has shown me how to age up with endless adventure and joy. She is my role model who goes through everything first.

To all of my mentor friends who were in their 40s when we met 30 years ago and are still teaching me as we grow: Brian Campbell, Jackie St. Joan, Kathy Bowers, and the late Jill Cobb and Jeanne Elliott.

To Laurie Draft, my extraordinary editor and Lisa Monias my great designer — they are the BEST partners on a project.

To my parents and aunts and uncles, all of whom are gone, because they showed such grace and courage as they faced the indignities and challenges of late-life aging.

To my friends as we go through these challenges together.

Thanks to my agent, Vincent Marcus of the VJM Agency, and my editors, Amy Hall and Christine York at Newhouse Books.

Finally, thanks to you for buying this book. I hope your days and years are filled with adventure, joy, and hope—no matter what.

Work Directly
with Fawn Germer

What If Your Best Years
Haven't Even Happened Yet?

Retirement isn't the end of the road—it's the beginning of a brand-new journey. Sometimes, navigating your newfound freedom can be overwhelming. That's where best-selling author Fawn Germer comes in. Fawn is a life coach for people who haven't quite found their footing in retirement and want to design a life filled with more fun, excitement, and purpose.

Fawn is revered for her direct approach to living. Her coping model of "Accept. Cope. Adapt." has helped tens of thousands of men and women face life and find their way. She is the best-selling author of 11 books, including an Oprah book. She is cohost of the top Hard Won Wisdom Podcast and a four-time Pulitzer Prize nominee.

For information, write info@fawngermer.com or call (727) 467-0202.

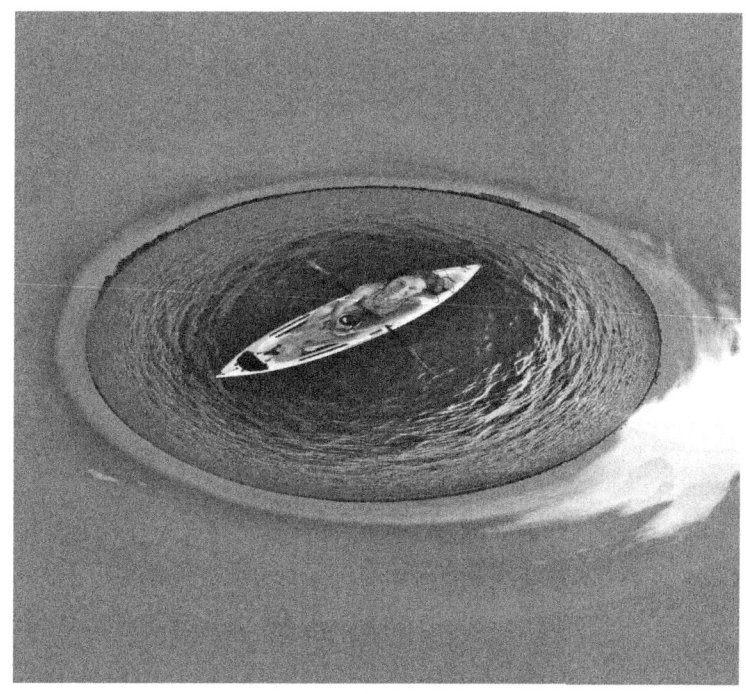

About Fawn

Fawn Germer is the best-selling author of eleven books and has been the motivational keynote speaker for nearly 100 Fortune 500 companies. Her first career, as an investigative reporter, resulted in four nominations for the Pulitzer Prize. Her first book, rejected everywhere, was an Oprah book.

Enough of that.

Fawn is a kayaker, dog lover, hiker, cyclist, swimmer, camper, stargazer, sunrise lover, sunset addict, good friend, and a somewhat introverted, generally happy person who lives in Dunedin, Florida with her dog Sonny and two cats, Coconut and Teddy. She loves big water, blue skies, tall trees, all things outdoors, and classic rock (especially the Rolling Stones).

For coaching and speaking information, write info@fawngermer.com, visit fawngermer.com, or call 727-467-0202.

Printed in Great Britain
by Amazon

58943013R00117